melt

The Art of Macaroni and Cheese

melt

The Art of Macaroni and Cheese

Stephanie Stiavetti & Garrett McCord

Foreword by Michael Ruhlman
Photographs by Matt Armendariz

LITTLE, BROWN AND COMPANY
NEW YORK   BOSTON   LONDON

Little, Brown and Company
Hachette Book Group
237 Park Avenue, New York, NY 10017
littlebrown.com

First Edition: October 2013

Little, Brown and Company is a division of Hachette Book Group, Inc.
The Little, Brown name and logo are trademarks of Hachette Book Group, Inc.

The publisher is not responsible for websites (or their content) that are not
owned by the publisher.

The Hachette Speakers Bureau provides a wide range of authors for speaking
events. To find out more, go to hachettespeakersbureau.com or call
(866) 376-6591.

Photographs on pages ix, 4, 9, 10, 192–93, and 199 copyright © 2013
Stephanie Stiavetti.

ISBN 978-0-316-21337-0
Library of Congress Control Number 2013935275

10 9 8 7 6 5 4 3 2 1

SC

Book and jacket design by Gary Tooth/Empire Design Studio

Printed in China

To our partners, Brian and Thadeus. Hearts of gold. Stomachs of steel.

To our parents, for their lifelong support and for making us the passionate, driven food writers we've become. Endless appreciation to Suzanne McCord, Michael McCord, Carole Stiavetti, Robert Stiavetti, and Michele Stiavetti.

CONTENTS

FOREWORD
MICHAEL RUHLMAN

In all of my work, I've tried to simplify cooking. Seeing a fancy-schmancy recipe for, oh, I don't know, Chocolate Pasta with Bucherondin, Hazelnuts, and Cherries, I'd think, so, basically mac and cheese, right?

Stephanie Stiavetti and Garrett McCord, dynamic writers and committed, inventive cooks, have gone the other way, taking a simple idea and looking at it from dozens of different angles (such as that astonishing chocolate pasta I just mentioned, page 44; *epic*, as Steph would say). They've put their imagination and intelligence into exploring those seemingly simple components and explaining how they work and why, and how to use them best, making this book really a primer in cheeses as well as a concise lesson in the multitudes of pasta and best ways of cooking them.

I have to admit that when Stephanie and Garrett told me their first cookbook was about macaroni and cheese, I groaned inwardly. It wasn't because I don't love a good mac and cheese, an American classic. I put a recipe for one of my own in my last book. But a hundred different casseroles of basically the same thing? So it was first with relief ("Oh, thank God"), and then rapt attention ("I did not know that!"), that I entered this delightful and fascinating treatment of a single idea: combining pasta and cheese, and all that we might make of it.

Yes, there are plenty of macaroni and cheese casseroles (I've already decided what I'm making for dinner tonight, the Lincolnshire Poacher, page 115!), but *Melt* proposes a wide range of ingenious combinations of pasta and cheese, a union that is, by the way, found in almost every food culture, and not unique to the United States. We may call it macaroni and cheese, but the authors show us in recipes, photographs, and words how amazingly diverse this fundamental combination can be (I love their chapter on salads, for instance). Foremost, Stephanie and Garrett ask us to consider a variety of high-quality cheeses to replace the default generic Cheddar or mozzarella called for in most mac-and-cheese recipes.

I still remember a fifth-grade field trip to Ohio's Amish country, where I bought some genuine Swiss cheese. It was so good I nearly couldn't believe it. It was a great mystery, and an introduction of sorts to the strangeness of my own country: this cheese, this marvel, was the same as that sliced and collated cheese in the bright plastic vacuum-sealed bag dangling from the metal hook at the grocery store? How could it be?

It would be twenty years before I had cheese as good and understood why: that 1972 Swiss cheese had been made by the family that raised the cows. Twenty years later there would be an amazing farmers' market near my house where local cheesemakers sold their cheeses.

We are of course in the midst of a food renaissance in the United States. Never has there been a better time to be a cook or an eater. One facet of the renaissance is the extraordinary cheeses we have begun to create, from coast to coast. This agriculturally rich country today produces some of the best cheeses *in the world*. And Stephanie and Garrett offer outstanding information on America's cheeses; this and their recommendations are worth the price of the book.

I know of no better, simpler lunch than a great cheese, a piece of baguette, and a glass of wine. But sometimes that's all we think of when we spend money on a good cheese: putting it on a cutting board. Stephanie and Garrett are now asking us to think about the range of cheeses available, and *cooking* with them, combining them with pasta in unique ways—and their recipes are swooningly good. They ask us to consider the unique qualities of cheeses made from goat's milk, cow's milk, and sheep's milk. Cheese from goat's milk tends to be tangy and often pleasantly barnyard-y, while sheep's milk is especially fatty, and so each works differently in food.

But there's a bigger message in this book. For half my life, the macaroni and cheese this country knew came out of a box and included powder with orange food coloring—if I ate it, I don't remember. I still see busy parents serving it to their young children. This cheap dinner in a box epitomizes the travesty of America's processed-food industry and the damage it has wrought on the people who rely on it and on our land.

This book is a personal reminder to me to appreciate real food. I love to cook, and elaborate recipes and preparations don't scare me. I actively criticize the media for continually hunting for the "quick and easy" recipe rather than the good one. But it's true that life is busy, and sometimes we simply don't have the time to spend an hour on a weeknight to create a healthful, balanced, delicious meal for our family. Given some good cheese, milk, and dried pasta, you are literally minutes from an astonishingly delicious meal. Want simple? Try the Surfing Goat Chèvre with Cherry Tomatoes, Spinach, Dill, and Gemelli (page 65, works great with any quality chèvre, of course). Want to impress your friends? Try the Buffalo Chicken Macaroni with Buttermilk Blue Cheese Sauce (page 157). That's even fun to say!

I'm writing this on a chilly fall day, a Saturday, when I will have as much time as I choose to spend in the kitchen. I'm still going to make that mac-and-cheese casserole. I'll pair it with a kale salad for satisfying nutrition and bite and fiber, but it's the macaroni and cheese I've already started looking forward to that will be the centerpiece of the dinner table.

melt

The Art of Macaroni and Cheese

CHAPTER 1:
THE BASICS

CHAPTER 1:
THE BASICS

There's an

American myth that Thomas Jefferson invented macaroni and cheese; that he sat on his porch at Monticello, his private plantation, and ate heaping bowls of it with his family. The truth, however, is that Jefferson was more of an ambassador for macaroni and cheese than its inventor. During trips to France and Italy he became utterly fascinated by the many varieties of pasta, from tiny spirals and wavy-ridged sheets to frilly bow ties and spoked wagon wheels. He marveled at the extrusion process and the machines that were able to produce incredible amounts of pasta in a short time. He eventually began importing pasta, cheese, and his own extruders to Monticello, where he served macaroni and cheese at state dinners.

Macaroni and cheese has been an American obsession ever since. The dish spread like wildfire through the South, as it provided an economical, hearty, and flavorful way to fill oneself up using local farmstead cheese. It's now a staple on almost any soul-food menu. Mary Randolph, one of America's first cookbook authors and sister to Thomas Mann Randolph Jr., son-in-law to Thomas Jefferson, wrote one of the earliest American recipes for macaroni and cheese, which called for only butter, pasta, and cheese, layered and baked. Ernest Hemingway is said to have adored the dish and ate it throughout Europe; Henry, Hemingway's main character in *A Farewell to Arms*, eats it during a bombardment, the dish representing grace and calm amid the chaos of war. A rather insightful observation about macaroni and cheese, don't you think?

Of course, macaroni and cheese existed in many forms before it came to mean so much to the very young country of the United States. The Italians, for example, served pasta with sun-dried tomatoes and salty shavings of Parmesan, as well as dishes of lasagna packed with ricotta. The Swiss baked pasta with layers of melty Gruyère, the local mountain cheese. The French, no strangers to macs of all kinds, stirred any cheese they could find into their many mother sauces. Even in places far from modern Western culture, like Tibet and Mexico, pasta and cheese have long greeted each other warmly on piping-hot plates.

ABOUT CHEESE

CHEESE HAS A RICH AND VARIED HISTORY THAT STRETCHES back to six thousand years before the birth of Christ. Not surprisingly, the most ancient cheeses were created by early agrarian civilizations. These early cheeses were likely made from sheep's or goat's milk and took the form of fresh, acid-coagulated cheeses, like ricotta, or brined cheeses, like feta. Over time, whether through trial and error or simple accident, many cultures began to discover ways to make, preserve, and flavor cheese, such as wrapping it in leaves, aging it in caves, or controlling the growth of certain molds that enhanced the flavors of the milk.

Due to the ravages of time, a lack of written records, and historical events such as war and migration, many cheesemaking recipes have been lost over the ages. In relatively recent history, for example, World Wars I and II resulted in the extinction of several types, as resources in many European countries went to churning out only hard cheeses that could stay on a shelf and sleep for years, like Rip Van Winkle. As a result, many varieties of cheese vanished forever.

Thankfully, many artisan cheesemakers with a passion for good cheese persevered and kept their traditions alive, and we have a wealth of European cheeses to enjoy as a result. The United States experienced a renaissance of fine cheesemaking in the 1970s and 1980s, and a recent revolution of artisan and farmstead cheesemaking has produced varieties that rival those in Europe.

Today there are more cheesemakers than ever to complement the growing number of consumers with adventurous palates, hungry individuals who are excited to explore these new offerings. While many still feel that artisan cheese should be placed on a pedestal, worshipped like a fermented deity, and eaten without any accoutrements or condiments, others are learning to experience cheese in new ways, pairing it with beers, layering it between slices of bread, or using it to craft exquisite varieties of macaroni and cheese.

HOW CHEESE IS MADE

AT A SCIENTIFIC, MICROSCOPIC LEVEL, THE CHEESEMAKING process is quite complicated and involves a solid understanding of chemistry and biology. Milk, produced by mammals to nourish their young, is one of the earth's most complex foods. A mixture of fats, proteins, nutrients, sugars, water, and a number of beneficial bacteria, milk is essentially a vital organism, a living, breathing thing. So is cheese. Once fresh milk has been collected and stored, the cheesemaking process can begin.

The first step in cheesemaking is for the milk to acidify and coagulate. Bacterial cultures and acid agents can be added to the milk to assist in the process, or the milk can be left to acidify and ripen on its own. These cultures and acids will later shape a cheese's textures and flavors, but initially

These baby goats may one day join their mothers in making great cheese.

their job is to convert lactose, milk's natural sugar, to lactic acid. The more a cheese ages, the less lactic acid it contains. (If you are lactose intolerant, aged cheeses can be somewhat easier to digest.) Next, rennet is added to encourage coagulation: the breakdown of milk proteins and their reconfiguration into solids (curds) that break apart from the liquid (whey).

The curds are then cut and heated. They may be cooked hard, or warmed slowly to expel more whey. This is a critical juncture for cheese, as the temperature and texture of the curds can affect the final product. For example, the more the curds are cut and cooked, the firmer and drier they will be, resulting in a harder cheese with less moisture.

The curds are then placed into molds, baskets, or other holders so they can be drained and formed into a more unified mass. Some are simply compressed by their own weight, while others require additional weight to be placed on top to compress them, creating a firmer texture. Not all cheeses are pressed, though.

The cheese is then salted and put through the rigors of additional treatments and aging. These treatments can include the inoculation of various molds (to create blue cheeses), wrapping in leaves or bark, rubbing with wine, and a number of other finishings. The cheese then continues to ripen and develop the pronounced flavors that make it so delectable.

TYPES OF MILK

- **COW'S MILK—**Cows produce more milk than goats or sheep, which allows a cheesemaker to produce a great deal of cheese per milking. The flavors are beefier and more buttery than those of other milks, and the cheeses generally contain less fat. They can be harder to digest due to the fact that their milk solids are so large, and they have almost triple the amount of milk proteins that human milk has.

SALT AND CHEESE

SALT—AN IMPORTANT COMPOUND MINERAL in the human diet—is crucial to the making of fine cheese. One of the reasons cheese tastes the way it does is the addition of salt at various stages of the cheesemaking process. While salt enhances the natural flavors of the milk, it also plays an important role in a cheese's development. Salt can be added using a wet method, in which the cheese is dunked into a brining solution; this results in a washed-rind cheese (see sidebar The Sweet World of Stinky Cheeses—The Source of the Smell, page 145). Salt can also be added to cheese using one of two dry methods. It can be put into the curds before pressing, which quickly halts bacterial activity, or it can be rubbed on the surface of the cheese after pressing, which results in a more mature rind, as it pulls out moisture from the curd.

Salt's primary duty in cheesemaking is to control moisture content. It may not sound like much, but moisture levels are critical when it comes to developing a cheese's personality. Water content dictates how soft or hard a cheese will be and how long the bacteria in the cheese can continue the fermentation process. This, in turn, determines the pH level, or how strong a bite the cheese will have.

When applied to the outside of a cheese, salt also helps in the development of the rind. It draws moisture from the cheese, so the outside surface will dry out more quickly, resulting in a tougher, harder coating. In a washed-rind cheese, salt assists in the proper development of the famously stinky *Brevibacterium linens* bacteria.

- **GOAT'S MILK**—The tangy, flavorful milk of goats is often used to make fresh and soft cheeses. Goat cheese frequently has a chalkier texture than cheeses made from other milks, with a tart flavor profile. Goat's milk produces hints of old wood, grass, wet stone, and black pepper, and barnyard-like flavors.

- **SHEEP'S MILK**—Milk from ewes contains more fat, protein, and milk solids than either goat's or cow's milk. This means that the milk can better tolerate heat treatments and freezing, and it's better suited for the needs of cheesemaking. These cheeses also have more pronounced flavor than cow's milk and pair well with other ingredients. Flavors are often grassy and nutty, with distinct overtones of hay. Sheep produce less milk than goats or cows, but their milk has more butterfat and protein solids, so it yields more cheese per quart.

- **OTHER MILKS**—Milk from any number of animals is used throughout the world to make cheese. Water buffalo produce exceptional milk for fresh cheese, and the milk is becoming widely used in Europe and North America. In Tibet, yaks are more common than cattle and are used for their bones, skins, meat, and milk, the last often made into various types of cheese. In Egypt, it's not unusual to find cheeses made from camel's milk. Llama cheeses have small fan clubs here and there. These cheeses are not generally available for purchase in Europe and North America, though, so if you get the chance to try one, don't pass up the opportunity!

- **MIXED MILK**—The milk from multiple types of animals can be mixed to produce some wonderfully complex cheeses. The beneficial qualities of each type of milk blend to create unique flavors and textures.

TYPES OF CHEESE

THERE ARE MANY WAYS TO CATEGORIZE CHEESE, THE MOST popular being by texture, or bite, as this provides a point of reference to the age of the cheese and its overall characteristics. Other categories describe a cheese's unique properties and processes. There are also a number of subcategories of cheese, such as smoked, ash-ripened, and wrapped, and many fall into multiple categories. For the sake of the recipes in this book, let's discuss cheeses in terms of how they cook.

- **FRESH, SOFT**—These cheeses are freshly made and quite young, with little to no aging. Some—like feta and chèvre—crumble but don't melt, due to their protein structure and method of coagulation. Others, like fromage blanc and ricotta, do melt, but they won't thread when cooked.

- **PASTA FILATA**—An Italian term meaning "spun paste" that refers to cheeses that thread. Threading is most frequently associated with dry, low-moisture mozzarella and burrata: When you bite into a piece of cooked cheese and long strings of it stretch from your mouth, well, that's threading (string cheese is one aptly named example). These cheeses are made by massaging and stretching the curds as they bathe in hot whey.

- **SOFT-RIPENED AND SURFACE-RIPENED**—These cheeses, such as Brie, Humboldt Fog, and Camembert, are only a few months old and have a high moisture content. With some, molds form on the outside of the cheese, resulting in a soft, pliable rind—hence the term *bloomy-rind cheese*. These cheeses melt beautifully, but you won't get any threading; instead, they'll meld delicately into a sauce. In some cases, they can act as sauces on their own.

- **SEMISOFT**—Alpine cheeses, some washed-rind cheeses, some Cheddars, and many other varieties fall into this category. When heat is applied to them directly, they melt well but retain some of their structure and shape (think of how you can sometimes see the shape of each individual shred of cheese on a pizza). They melt into a sauce with ease if you give them a little help with a wooden spoon and a bit of stirring. Overheating may cause them to clump and break, so remove your sauce from the heat before stirring in the shredded cheese.

- **WASHED-SOFT**—Think of cheeses like Taleggio, Nicasio Square, and Red Hawk. These are slick on the outside, oozy on the inside, and stinky all over. The washing solution the cheeses are bathed in can be composed of anything from spirits to a briny saline solution. Although you can eat the rind, it's definitely a personal choice. Some love it, and some don't. Washed-rind cheeses have a tendency to get oozy when ripe; some partially retain their shape when cooked, while others melt into an almost saucelike consistency. Beware of excessively slimy rinds, as they may indicate a cheese past its prime. When in doubt, ask your cheesemonger.

- **HARD CHEESES**—An intense, crystalline structure and a salty flavor profile define hard cheeses. More often than not, these are used for grating or for flavoring dishes, though a chunk by itself can be delightful. The pleasing crunchy crystals are a natural part of the aging process, produced when chains of amino acids break down (see Little Fireworks, next page). Think of Piave, Pecorino Romano, and Parmesan; these cheeses are best finely shredded before cooking, as they resist melting, though they will melt into a mornay sauce if well mixed. They also make for a fabulous casserole topping when tossed with breadcrumbs.

- **BLUE CHEESES**—Cheese lore says that blue cheese was an accident. As the story goes, a shepherd left some forgotten bread sitting in his aging cave next to his cheese. When he returned a few weeks later, *bam*, the now moldy bread had infected the cheese. The shepherd tried it, loved it, and the rest is history. These cheeses are now carefully crafted; each cheese is pierced by stainless-steel needles to encourage airflow through-

out the cheese, bringing oxygen to the mold spores with which the cheese is inoculated. Blue cheeses can be hard, semisoft, or even fresh and will cook accordingly. When you melt blue cheeses alongside other ingredients in a dish, they can leave behind their molds in alluring veins of spicy flavor that lace the food. After cooking, blues can become even more peppery.

CHEESE PRODUCTION TERMINOLOGY

HERE IS A QUICK SET OF DEFINITIONS THAT WILL HELP YOU better understand the cheeses you're buying and eating.

- **INDUSTRIAL OR MASS-PRODUCED CHEESE**—High-output factories produce the cheese with milk that comes from a large number of farms.

- **SPECIALTY CHEESE**—Produced with less mechanization than mass-produced cheese. Cheese is made in smaller amounts but is not considered "handmade."

- **ARTISAN CHEESE**—An individual producer crafts the cheese with milk from various farms. Artisan cheeses are often considered "handmade."

- **COOPERATIVE CHEESE**—An individual dairy makes cheese from milk that comes from a number of cooperative farms. Cooperative cheeses *can* be considered artisan or specialty as well.

- **FARMSTEAD CHEESE**—A dairy farm produces the cheese from the milk of its own animals. Many farmstead cheeses are also artisan cheeses, as they are often handmade in small batches.

Other terms such as *raw, organic*, and *sustainable* may be used, but these terms are defined by local laws and can have many interpretations. Ask your cheesemaker or cheesemonger for clarification if you're unsure what these terms mean as they pertain to a particular cheese.

LITTLE FIREWORKS

IF YOU'VE EVER CHOMPED DOWN ON A PIECE of well-aged Cheddar or Parmesan, you've no doubt encountered a strange textural sensation. Within the cheese are crystalline bits that spark and shatter in your mouth like tiny flecks of glass. These little fireworks are tyrosine, an amino-acid by-product of aging cheese. The name comes from the Greek word *tyros*, which means "cheese."

Casein is a phosphoprotein—a protein containing chemically bound phosphoric acid—found in milk, and thus in cheese. Proteins trap fats and sugars during the cheesemaking process. As a cheese ages, some of these chains break down. Tyrosine, a component of casein, is a by-product of these broken chains, and deposits of it form tiny crystals.

These crystals are harmless and create a sense of textural vivacity within the cheese. Tyrosine crystals should not be confused with salt crystals, which sometimes form on the rinds of brined cheeses. Pockets of salty liquid can collect in crevices on a cheese's surface during the brining process, leaving chunks of salt behind after the brine has evaporated.

HOW TO PURCHASE CHEESE

BUYING CHEESE IS ONE OF THE MOST ENJOYABLE ASPECTS of the artisan cheese experience. The awe that overcomes you as you gaze into an expansive and sagely composed cheese case should be reveled in. Of course, it can be daunting too, as you'll undoubtedly encounter any number of cheeses with quirky or foreign names, like Fat Bottom Girl or Chabichou du Poitou. Which cheese is which, and what cheeses are right for you?

To begin with, you need to find a good cheese shop. Many fine-food stores and some large supermarkets now have well-stocked cheese counters and a dedicated cheesemonger. A cheesemonger is the person who buys, ages, cuts, sells, and instructs customers about cheese. The first thing you should do is introduce yourself to the cheesemonger and become his or her friend. The cheesemonger wants to take care of you, educate you, answer your questions, and ensure you have a practically perfect cheese experience. If you are excited about cheese, odds are your cheesemonger will appreciate your enthusiasm and treat you with respect.

Now comes the tantalizing part of shopping for cheese: tasting. If a cheese counter won't allow you to try before you buy, take your business elsewhere. You need to be able to taste a cheese to see if it is to your liking before you purchase it. If you're looking for a particular cheese that isn't in stock, the cheesemonger may be able to special-order the one you want or offer an alternative.

These days you can also go online and order cheese from major vendors, such as Artisanal and Murray's, or buy directly from the cheesemakers or other smaller shops with online stores. You obviously can't try before you buy with online purchases, and in many cases you will have to pay for special packaging and overnight delivery, as cheese can spoil en route if not shipped properly. Despite this limitation, it can be a great way to try new cheeses that might otherwise be hard to come by.

STORING CHEESE

CHEESE IS A LIVING THING. THE BACTERIA AND MOLDS IN cheese need oxygen in order to breathe. If you wrap the cheese up in plastic wrap, it may suffocate and spoil.

You can buy specialty cheese paper for wrapping your cheese, which helps control the moisture content (as refrigeration can dry cheese out) and allows the cheese to breathe, though wrapping cheese in parchment paper will work just fine. Don't panic if you don't have any parchment or cheese paper; Tupperware will work for a few days too.

Some cheeses can live in the refrigerator for quite a while and still be delicious, taking on new flavors and textures as they continue to ripen. But if your cheese grows a large amount of foreign molds or begins to smell like ammonia, it may have gone the way of the zombie. You can remove a small amount of surface mold with a sharp knife, but if your cheese has been taken over by colorful flora, let it rest in peace...in the garbage. Some cheeses are purposely crafted to take on a slightly ammoniated smell, but often the odor of ammonia is a bad sign. When in doubt, a quick call to your cheesemonger is always a good idea.

Note: *Be sure to store blue cheese away from other cheeses. The mold can jump ship and colonize nearby cheeses, interacting with other bacteria and milks in unpredictable ways. While this may sound like the chance to create new, novel cheeses at home, you'll likely be disappointed by the results.*

A well-stocked cheese counter is worth its weight in dairy gold.

After you find a cheese you like, you can buy either a precut piece that's been priced by weight or a fresh piece cut from the cheese wheel. Cheeses are almost always sold by weight. Online they are often sold in half-pound (eight-ounce) increments.

Many cheesemakers also sell their cheeses at local farmers' markets. This is a chance to meet the dairy crafters directly and get more information about their animals and cheeses. They can also provide you with samples and ideas of how best to enjoy their cheeses. Plus, they can tell you a great cheese joke or two. They're whey good at those.

EXPERIENCING CHEESE

EXPERIENCING CHEESE IS SO MUCH MORE THAN JUST noticing how it tastes. If you pay close attention, you may be surprised at how many senses cheese connects with.

- **SIGHT**—Your eyes are among the most reliable tools for identifying cheese. Each cheese has its own look, and while some may appear similar to one another, they all have distinct visual characteristics that make them unique. Shape, texture, pattern, color, and type of rind are the best ways to identify a cheese.

- **TOUCH**—Pick up a cheese and feel how dense it is. Run your fingers around the rind. Does it dent, bounce back, or resist you when you poke it? Is it pasty or crumbly? Does it fall with a thud, or can you bounce it off your friend's forehead? Be familiar with what good cheeses feel like so you can tell when one is past its prime.

- **SMELL**—When it comes to cheese, smell and taste are not always related. Take a piece of Taleggio, for example—the smell is odiferous and funky, while the flavor is beefy and mellow. A cheese's smell is unique, though a cheese that smells strongly of ammonia is sometimes one to avoid. If you're unsure, ask.

- **TASTE**—The most important (and fun) way to experience cheese is obviously by taste. Take a piece and let it cover your entire tongue. Notice how the flavor may vary from the interior of the cheese to the part closest to the rind. Is it nutty? Sulfury? Grassy? Mushroomy? Does it have a spicy bite or prickle the tongue? Does it fall into one or many of the five taste categories (bitter, salty, sour, sweet, and savory/umami)?

Keep in mind that cheeses will display different characteristics and properties when paired with other flavors. Food and drink will greatly affect the way you experience a cheese, possibly highlighting or hiding certain characteristics. In fact, a cheese may take on entirely new qualities when paired just right. Pairings helped guide the crafting of the recipes in this book; particular ingredients were chosen to highlight each cheese's most stunning qualities.

Just like fruits and vegetables, cheeses go in and out of season. The diet of the animals that produce the milk often changes depending on the time of year, from fresh grass in spring to dry straw in the winter. This changes the flavor profile of the milk, and therefore of the cheese.

Your cheesemonger likely has a lot of inspiring cheeses to share.

HOW TO SHRED CHEESE

A GOOD NUMBER OF THE RECIPES IN THIS BOOK CALL FOR shredded cheese, and there are many ways to accomplish this simple task. First, it's important to know that cold cheese shreds better than room-temperature cheese, since the fat is in a more solid state and won't turn to mush when you apply pressure to it. Also, cold cheese is less likely to gum up and melt into a large mass once it's been shredded. Unless otherwise specified, do yourself a favor and keep your cheese in the refrigerator until it's ready to be chopped.

- **CHEESE GRATERS**—Perhaps the most familiar method for shredding cheese is to use a cheese grater. You can use any kind of grater you like, from a plane slicer to a fancy box model. We recommend using one with larger holes, as this will make the shredding process much faster and more efficient.

- **FOOD PROCESSORS**—While it can be an experience in Zen meditation to grate your cheese by hand, you can also cut cheese into one-inch cubes and toss them into a food processor, then make short work of the grating process with a few quick pulses. Be aware that hard cheeses will shred easily, but some stickier cheeses will force your food processor to work harder. If your appliance starts sounding like it's running the last leg of an ultramarathon, give the motor a rest for ten to fifteen minutes before shredding any more cheese. Chilling your cheese before shredding will make it easier for your food processor to chop effectively.

- **KNIVES**—If you do not own a cheese grater or food processor, you can always use a knife and a cutting board to reduce the cheese to small chunks. A note of caution: Use a sharp knife, but always be aware of where the blade is moving. If the knife sticks within the body of the cheese, do not force it. Carefully remove the knife from its stuck position and restart the cut. Your tender digits will thank you (as the authors can personally attest!).

SHOULD YOU REMOVE THE RIND?

ONE QUESTION WE'RE OFTEN ASKED IS, "SHOULD I REMOVE the rind from my cheese before cooking with it?" The answer: Maybe; it depends. Many cheeses come encased in a coating of hard wax, which you'll want to remove and discard before shredding. The rinds of washed-rind cheeses are beloved by some and despised by others. Some people eat the leaves of a leaf-wrapped cheese, while others don't much care for them. In other words, if the rind is edible, it's totally up to you whether or not you add it to the dish.

In most of our recipes, we've indicated in the ingredient list whether the rind should be removed or shredded with the rest of the cheese, but in some cases it really is your call. Wax rinds should always be removed. (Unless you really like eating wax, we suppose.) We encourage you to experiment and explore the wonders of the rind. How does it taste? Do you enjoy the texture? Does it have a flavor that dissipates quickly or lingers on the tongue? While we make recommendations about whether or not to remove the rind, if you love the rind of a particular cheese, you're more than welcome to add it to the recipe.

Feel free to play with rinds in other ways as well. For example, did you know that you can steep Parmesan rinds to create a flavorful broth, as in our recipe for Swiss Chard, Rotini, and Cannellini Beans in Parmesan Broth (page 109)? Play. Explore. Learn.

ABOUT PASTA

WE HAVE DEVOTED A LOT OF SPACE TO DISCUSSING THE particulars of cheese, but we'd be remiss if we didn't pay proper respect to the macaroni component of macaroni and cheese. Pasta is the kind of food that isn't given a lot of thought unless it's done wrong—and then it's a real problem—so remember that noodles are the second-most-important element in any macaroni and cheese recipe.

PURCHASING PASTA

MANY FOLKS HIT THE GROCERY STORE AND BUY WHATEVER brand of pasta is on sale. This is not necessarily a bad thing, but what you want to keep in mind when buying pasta is its freshness. You may not have noticed, but most packages of pasta have an expiration date. You can eat pasta that is past its prime, but for optimal flavor and texture, make sure you're buying and preparing pasta that has a relatively distant expiration date—and if given the choice, avoid brands that eschew the expiration date altogether.

WHY CHOOSE PREMIUM DRIED PASTA?

AS AN INGREDIENT, DRIED PASTA IS RELATIVELY LOW maintenance and easy to produce. That said, there are countless brands and styles out there, ranging from run-of-the-mill one-dollar supermarket brands to high-quality varieties that cost as much as twenty dollars a pound. Cheap pasta will work just fine for the recipes in this book, though there's something to be said for investing in premium noodles. Artisan pastas are often made from higher-quality wheat and have a rougher texture that gives sauce something extra to hang on to, and those that are slow dried will have a fresher, nuttier flavor than those that are flash dried. Once you try a bite of truly great pasta, you may have a hard time going back to eating whatever's on sale at the grocery store.

Here are a few brands of dried artisan pasta that we recommend (in no particular order):

* **RUSTICHELLA D'ABRUZZO**
* **PAPPARDELLE'S**
* **BAIA PASTA**
* **PASTA LATINI**
* **CAVALIERE GIUSEPPE COCCO**
* **CIPRIANI**
* **LUNDBERG (GLUTEN-FREE)**

STORING PASTA

REGARDLESS OF WHAT KIND OF PASTA YOU USE, YOU WANT it to taste as fresh as possible. Wheat contains a good amount of oil, and when pasta is not stored properly, the oil goes rancid and can drastically affect the flavor of your noodles (and, of course, your overall dish). To ensure its optimal freshness, pasta should be stored in a sealed container, away from heat and light. A closed pantry makes a great storage place, as does a drawer, a closet, or a kitchen cabinet. If you're buying premium pasta, consider keeping it in the refrigerator or freezer if you're planning on storing it for longer than a few weeks.

SPECIAL COOKING TOOLS AND IMPLEMENTS

MAKING MACARONI AND CHEESE DOESN'T GENERALLY require any special tools, though there are some implements that may make your cooking experience easier or more enjoyable. Here are a few pieces of kitchen equipment you might consider adding to your collection if you don't already own them.

BAKING DISHES, CASSEROLE DISHES, RAMEKINS, AND MINI-COCOTTES

MANY OF THE RECIPES IN THIS BOOK CALL FOR SPECIFIC baking dishes, though in the end, these recipes aren't nearly that picky. Baking dishes are the same you might use to make brownies (an 8-by-8-inch or 9-by-9-inch pan) or lasagna (a 9-by-13-inch pan). We specify pan size in individual recipes and recommend using ceramic or glass, as they retain heat and cook more evenly than their stainless-steel counterparts.

Casserole dishes come in a number of sizes and shapes, though in our recipes we use casserole dishes that are roughly four quarts unless otherwise specified. Anything around that size will work well, and you also have the option of splitting the recipe in two if smaller dishes are all you have.

Gratin dishes are similar to casserole dishes, though you'll usually find them elliptical in shape and more shallow than other styles of cookware. In the absence of a gratin dish, a casserole dish or baking dish will work just fine.

Ramekins and mini-cocottes are simply small baking dishes. They come in a huge variety of sizes and shapes, so we specify which to use in individual recipes. As long as they are the same size, ramekins can be substituted for mini-cocottes, or vice versa.

STOVETOP COOKWARE

WHEN YOU'RE COOKING CHEESE ON THE STOVETOP, WE recommend using cookware that has a heavy bottom. This allows for even heat distribution and decreases the chances of burning the fragile milk sugars that live within dairy products. Heavy enameled cookware will give you excellent results, though pots and pans that have a bottom layer of aluminum sandwiched between sheets of stainless steel also work well. Thin metal cookware doesn't offer much of a shield between the heat and your cheese, so the cheese can scorch very quickly on the bottom of the pan. If you're using a pan of light construction, make sure to scrape the bottom frequently with a wooden spoon or flat-edge paddle.

OTHER TOOLS

THERE ARE A FEW OTHER TOOLS THAT ARE HANDY TO HAVE, though not necessary:

Wooden paddles are ideal for making thick sauces, such as béchamel and mornay. A paddle's flat head easily scrapes the bottom of the saucepan while you're cooking, and the square edges get into tight corners where sauce can collect and burn. Paddles are also perfect for folding pasta into cheese and stirring thick, melty casseroles.

It seems that there are as many styles of cheese knives as there are types of cheese. If you plan to be working with artisan cheeses on a regular basis, it makes sense to invest in a good set of cheese knives. Your local cheesemonger can likely recommend a set that he or she prefers and demonstrate the knives' proper uses.

A kitchen scale is a handy tool, whether you're measuring pasta, cheese, or other ingredients. It will give you far more accurate readings than any other method of measurement. We heartily recommend having one in your arsenal.

OTHER CONSIDERATIONS

BUYING AND MEASURING CHEESE BY WEIGHT

CHEESE COUNTERS SELL CHEESE BY WEIGHT. FOR EASE OF shopping, we've measured all cheeses by weight in the ingredient list for each recipe. A pound of cheese will weigh the same whether it's whole or shredded, and depending on how you shred your cheese, there can be huge differences in how much shredded cheese will fit into a measuring cup. For this reason, we don't offer volume measurements for the cheese in our recipes.

VISUALLY ESTIMATING THE WEIGHT OF CHEESE

WE RECOMMEND GETTING A GOOD KITCHEN SCALE SO YOU can measure the amount of cheese exactly before adding it to your dish. That said, there is a little flexibility in the amounts we've listed, so if a recipe calls for 8 ounces of cheese and you've got 7.6 or 8.8 ounces, that's fine. It's also acceptable to visually estimate based on weight. If you've bought three-quarters of a pound of cheese and a dish requires 8 ounces, you can visually estimate the two-thirds of your block of cheese that should go into the dish. If you're unsure of your visual math, get a scale. They can be purchased relatively inexpensively these days at places like Target and Walmart.

MEASURING PASTA BY WEIGHT

THE RECIPES IN THIS BOOK ALSO LIST PASTA BY WEIGHT. Like cheese, pasta is sold by weight, and volume can vary from brand to brand. A scale is useful in this regard, but visually estimating the amount of pasta for the recipe is fine. If your box of pasta is 16 ounces and the recipe calls for 8, you know to use half of the box.

ALTERNATIVE CHEESES

IN EACH RECIPE, WE LIST A HANDFUL OF ALTERNATIVE cheeses that will go well with the dish if you can't find the one we recommend. It's important to know that while an alternative cheese may be similar in flavor or style to the one in the recipe, the finished product may be very different. Our goal in providing alternatives was to make the recipe as solid as possible when using a different cheese; the alternative is not necessarily an exact match for the cheese originally called for.

WINE PAIRINGS

AT THE END OF EACH RECIPE IS A LIST OF WINE PAIRINGS that match both the cheese and the recipe as a whole. These are only recommendations; feel free to experiment with other wines, beers, and spirits.

FOOD PAIRINGS

WE BELIEVE YOU WILL LOVE THE CHEESES SELECTED FOR this book and you'll want to enjoy them in as many ways as possible. This is why you'll find a list of food pairings for each cheese at the end of each recipe. If you're interested in trying one of these cheeses on a cheese plate, these pairing suggestions will guide you in creating a balanced combination of flavors.

SEA SALT

WE RECOMMEND THAT YOU USE SEA SALT IN YOUR PASTA water and for seasoning your macaroni dishes, as sea salt has a more pure flavor and works well for our purposes. Kosher salt works fine as well. Flake salt, fleur de sel, or any other fine finishing salt will do, though these are expensive and might be best used for sprinkling over a dish once it's done. Please avoid using iodized salt, as it adds an unpleasant metallic flavor, and it can be difficult to gauge how much is enough.

READING AHEAD AND HAVING FAITH

WE URGE YOU TO READ EACH RECIPE COMPLETELY BEFORE
making it. This ensures you will have the required ingredients
and equipment at the ready and avoid surprises along the
way. There is nothing worse than realizing at step 5 that you
need to have another bowl ready and letting your cheese
burn while you scramble to find one.

Most important, a big part of cooking is having faith
in yourself. Your oven will not run the same as our ovens—
it will have quirks and hot spots that are unique to it. Your
"salting to taste" will be different than how we salt our food.
Whenever you cook, you place yourself in a state of agency
and confidence, and you must rely on your own sense and
judgment. Does the recipe look golden brown at 25 minutes
and not the recipe-recommended 35 minutes? Then take
it out! It's probably done. If it's not cooked through at 35
minutes, then let it cook a little longer. Have confidence in
your cooking abilities and treat everything as a learning
experience. We are not there with you (as much as we
would love to be). Taste, taste, taste each step of the way.
Check and double-check. Trust yourself. Trust your instincts.

A VERY BRIEF HISTORY OF PASTA

LEGEND HAS IT THAT MARCO POLO BROUGHT PASTA TO ITALY AFTER ONE OF HIS TREKS THROUGH China. However, the source of this legend is nothing more than a clever advertisement published in a 1929 trade periodical, *Macaroni Journal.*

Not that the Chinese didn't invent pasta. Over the millennia, they crafted many varieties, and noodles have been documented in Chinese history as far back as the Han dynasty in 206 BCE. The Chinese (as well as the Vietnamese, Hmong, Cantonese, and other Asian cultures) made not only wheat-and-water-based pasta—the pasta for which Italian cuisine is renowned—but also chewy egg noodles, sauce-loving lye-water noodles, wispy rice noodles, and many starch-based noodles, such as those made from mung beans.

The durum wheat pasta Americans are so familiar with was actually a creation of the ancient Arabs, who developed noodles in the fifth century as a staple food that could easily last through the travel of trade and conquest. In the eighth and ninth centuries, the Arabs occupied Sicily; it was here, in Palermo, Sicily's capital, that Sicilians adopted pasta as a basic staple in their diet. This was due to their occupation by the Arabs and the fact that hard-wheat cultivation exploded in the fair Mediterranean climate.

As pasta spread through the region, Italians began to refer to it as *macaroni,* a term derived from the Sicilian word for "making dough forcefully," as the dough had to be extruded through presses with a fair amount of effort. At the time, this was the general word for all pasta—not just the tiny elbows we know as macaroni today.

THE ORIGIN OF CHEESE

CHEESE IS AN ANCIENT FOOD; IT HAS EXISTED ALMOST AS LONG AS MANKIND HAS TENDED dairy animals. Records of fermented milk exist in the visual histories of the ancient Sumerians, Egyptians, Greeks, and Romans, dating back as far as 8000 to 6000 BCE.

How did cheese come about? As the story goes, people used the dried, leathery stomachs of slaughtered animals to carry milk from place to place, and since these animal stomachs contained traces of rennet, the enzyme-laden substance responsible for dairy coagulation, the milk turned to curds as the stomachs were jostled and shaken.

This was a very convenient discovery, as milk didn't keep for long in the pre-refrigeration days; solid cheese was easier to handle than milk and kept better in hot climates. Enzyme-based curdling enabled nomadic tribes to store dairy and carry it over long distances, a necessity for desert-dwelling civilizations.

However, ancient agrarian peoples had also been salting, brining, acidifying, and cooking milk in order to preserve their food, so cheese was actually a common discovery throughout the world. The earliest cheeses were generally fresh milk cheeses similar to cottage cheese or ricotta.

BASIC RECIPES

PREPARING YOUR PASTA WATER

WE'VE ALL BEEN TAUGHT DIFFERENT THINGS ABOUT HOW TO cook pasta properly. Lots of water or just enough? No salt, some salt, or as salty as the ocean? And let's not get into the great debate over whether you should add oil to the water, because people have come to blows over that.

Here is what we feel is the best way to prepare the pasta for our dishes. To begin, let's present you with the basic ratios:

» *1 quart of water should be used for every ¼ pound (4 ounces) of pasta*

This should ensure enough water to properly cover the pasta and allow the noodles plenty of room to float, bob, and swirl throughout the bubbling water for even cooking.

Next, we argue that you should always salt your water:

» *1 tablespoon of salt for every 2 quarts of water*

Salt brings out the flavor in the pasta and your overall dish. We believe that iodized salt should be avoided, as it has a processed, metallic flavor (try a dash by itself and see). Instead, we recommend that you use natural sea salt or kosher salt for the recipes in this book. If you have a sodium restriction in your diet, salt can be omitted.

Do not add salt before the water boils. Salt raises the boiling temperature of water, which will affect how well your pasta cooks. Instead, bring the water to a boil, add the salt, bring the water back to a boil, and add the noodles. Then cook the pasta as usual.

A lot of people say that adding oil to your cooking water prevents noodles from sticking together. This is not true. Oil just floats on top of the boiling water (remember, they don't mix) and any oil that does get on the pasta just slicks it up. You want your pasta starchy so that sauce sticks to the noodles, and oil causes your perfect sauce to slide right off.

As for rinsing your pasta in cool water after cooking, we recommend you don't do this unless the recipe specifically calls for it. You'll quickly lose those sticky, sauce-loving starches we mentioned above. Rinsing can also introduce extra, unnecessary water to your dish, which dilutes flavor and can make your noodles limp and soggy. We do instruct you in a few of our recipes to wash the pasta—so that it stays moist, or to get rid of the extra starch—but please resist the temptation otherwise.

MORNAY SAUCE

MANY PEOPLE HAVE HEARD OF BÉCHAMEL, A SIMPLE MILK sauce thickened with a butter-and-flour roux. Béchamel is a sauce that inexperienced home cooks often fear, though it's one of the easiest mother sauces to make. There are only three things in a basic béchamel: butter, flour, and warm milk. You melt some fat, add a little flour, and then stir in warm milk. Boom, that's it.

A mornay sauce is not very different; in fact, a mornay is simply a béchamel with cheese melted into its velvety depths. While it seems simple enough to fold cheese into a sauce, there's one caveat: You have to remove your sauce from its hot burner before you add the cheese. Why? It's a matter of chemistry: Cheese is a mixture of liquids and fat solids produced by curdling milk. When you heat curds, they may begin to separate. The easiest way to break your cheesy mornay sauce is to continue heating it as you stir in the cheese. If you remove your sauce from the heat source before adding the cheese, you'll achieve a gentler heating effect and lessen your chances of curdling.

A few tips on making perfect béchamel and mornay sauces:

• **USE UNSALTED BUTTER FOR THE ROUX AND FOLLOW** the directions in the recipe for the amount of salt and pepper to use. Add more salt and pepper to taste *after* you've stirred in the cheese, if you like.

• **MAKE SURE TO MEASURE YOUR FLOUR CAREFULLY. EVEN** a teaspoon too much flour can overthicken a sauce, making it impossible to pour.

- **WHEN COOKING A ROUX, BE SURE TO SCRAPE THE** bottom of the pan with a flat-head wooden paddle to keep it from burning. Wooden spoons do not work very well; you want something with a flat edge to evenly scrape all surfaces where the butter is cooking. If all else fails, use a heat-safe plastic spatula.

- **IF YOU BURN YOUR ROUX, TOSS IT AND START OVER.** You'll never get rid of that burned flavor.

- **USE YOUR EYES AND NOSE CAREFULLY WHEN COOKING** a roux. When you first add the flour to the butter and begin to stir, it will smell like raw flour and butter. As the roux cooks, it should darken in color and start to produce a nutty fragrance. That's when you add the milk—when it no longer smells raw but instead gives off a deeper, more complex fragrance. In other words, it should smell cooked.

- **USE WARM MILK, NOT BOILED MILK. BOILED MILK CAN** taste scorched, so we recommend keeping your milk in a pot on the stove over a burner at its lowest setting. When your milk is steaming and tiny bubbles have formed at the edges of the pan, it's at the correct temperature. Using cold milk might work in some cases, but you'll stand there stirring for twenty minutes while you wait for your milk to warm up and your sauce to thicken.

While there may be a few slight variations in the way we craft our mornay sauce in each recipe, here is the basic procedure:

MORNAY SAUCE

MAKES 2½ TO 3 CUPS OF SAUCE

- 2 tablespoons butter
- 2 tablespoons flour
- 2 cups warm milk (steaming, but not boiling)
- ½ teaspoon sea salt
- ¼ teaspoon freshly ground black pepper
- 10 ounces shredded cheese, such as Gruyère or a favorite Cheddar

1. Place the butter in a medium saucepan and melt over medium-low heat. Add the flour and stir with a wooden spatula for about 2 minutes, or just until the roux begins to turn a beige color and release a nutty aroma.

2. Add the warm milk, increase the heat to medium, and stir constantly until the sauce thickens enough to evenly coat the back of a spoon—a finger drawn along the back of the spoon should leave a clear swath. Add salt and pepper, and stir well. Remove from heat. Add cheese, one handful at a time, stirring constantly until completely melted. Serve immediately.

Incidentally, this sauce goes amazingly well with any number of things: potatoes, vegetables, chicken, and so forth. Mornay and béchamel sauces are not just for pasta!

MORNAY SAUCE WITH
GLUTEN-FREE ROUX

MACARONI-AND-CHEESE LOVERS OF THE GLUTEN-FREE persuasion likely already know that it's possible to swap regular wheat-based noodles for those made of rice, corn, quinoa, or any number of other grains. There remains, however, the problem of the roux we use in many recipes. What's a gluten-averse home cook to use in place of flour for thickening?

Thankfully, there is a simple alternative: sweet rice flour, also known as glutinous rice flour. Despite its name, this rice grain is, paradoxically, devoid of gluten compounds, and rice flour is safe for anyone with a gluten sensitivity. And it just so happens to make a very good roux. Huzzah! Just make sure you don't heat the butter too much before adding the flour, as sweet rice flour burns easily.

MAKES 2½ TO 3 CUPS OF SAUCE

2   **tablespoons butter**

2   **tablespoons sweet rice flour**
    (also known as glutinous rice flour)

2   **cups warm milk (steaming, not boiling)**

½   **teaspoon sea salt**

¼   **teaspoon freshly ground black pepper**

10 **ounces shredded cheese, such as Gruyère**
    or a favorite Cheddar

1. Place the butter in a medium saucepan and melt over medium-low heat. Do not overheat the butter, as rice flour particularly dislikes being overheated. Add the sweet rice flour to the butter and stir with a wooden spatula for about 1 minute, or just until the roux begins to take on a beige color and emit a nutty aroma.

2. Add the warm milk, increase the heat to medium, and stir until the sauce thickens. Add salt and pepper, and stir

well. Remove from heat, add cheese one handful at a time, stirring constantly until completely melted. Serve immediately over pasta (or veggies, potatoes, chicken, etc.).

IS BLUE CHEESE GLUTEN-FREE?

THERE IS SOME SPECULATION THAT BLUE cheese may not, in fact, be gluten-free. The concern arises from the fact that certain blue molds, such as *Penicillium roqueforti*, are grown on bread before they are added to milk during the cheesemaking process. While some people argue that there is not enough gluten in these varieties of blue cheese to affect someone with a sensitivity, there are also some gluten-sensitive folks who claim they've suffered serious consequences after eating certain blue cheeses.

So what's the truth? The answer is: It depends. Many large-production blue cheeses are likely gluten-free; if not, they will indicate within the ingredient list that the product may contain wheat. Many gluten-averse people confidently eat these varieties of blue cheese without concern. If in doubt, contact the manufacturer directly.

Artisan-produced cheeses, however, exist in more of a gray area. Many small-production cheeses are removed from their wrappers before being sold, so a consumer may never see the ingredient list. In these cases, we recommend asking your cheesemonger, who should have an intimate knowledge of his or her cheese selection and be able to speak to how the mold was grown. If the cheesemonger can't give you a satisfactory answer, it's perfectly acceptable to contact the cheesemaker yourself and ask for more information about the gluten status of a cheese.

A BIT ABOUT ALLERGY-FRIENDLY PASTA

AS MACARONI-AND-CHEESE RECIPE WRITERS, we've had many friends share the news that they've developed a food allergy to wheat or gluten. They tearfully recount the moment when they realized they would never eat pasta again. "Oh," they lament, "our culinary lives will be forever stunted!"

Okay, we're being facetious. The above scenario might have been the case twenty years ago, but thankfully here in the twenty-first century, there are countless allergen-free pastas available in most large-chain grocery stores. We've even seen gluten-free pasta on offer in small-town markets in sparsely populated areas. And if you can't find allergy-friendly pasta options in your area, there is a dizzying array of varieties available online at outlets like Amazon.com. Yes, really.

Do you have a gluten or wheat allergy? Never fear, there are many gluten-free pastas on the market of varying levels of mass production and artisan quality. Often made of brown-rice flour, these noodles are a little more sensitive to cooking but otherwise boil up very well. Rice pastas are perfectly lovely if treated with respect, but make sure you don't overcook them or you'll end up with an unsatisfying clump of sticky noodles. If rice isn't your thing, you'll also find pasta made from other starchy ingredients: corn, soy, quinoa, buckwheat, even seaweed and mung beans. No matter what kind of noodles you're cooking, the best advice is to follow the instructions on the package to a T. Preparation can vary from brand to brand, so listen to the good people who wrote the stuff on the box.

The flavors of some alternative-grain pastas go very well with cheese; others not so much. We recommend that you experiment and find out which pastas work best for each recipe. After many years of cooking with myriad kinds of allergy-friendly noodles, we believe that you can't go wrong with almost any brand of rice, corn, or quinoa noodles. Other types, such as fascinating—and tasty!—pastas made from vegetables and tubers, might require a little trial and error. And for what it's worth, yes, you can indeed create a gluten-free mornay sauce. We've even included a basic recipe to get you started on your way (see Mornay Sauce with Gluten-Free Roux, facing page). Aren't we thoughtful?

HOMEMADE BREADCRUMBS

AS INGREDIENTS GO, BREADCRUMBS DON'T USUALLY MERIT much thought. After all, they're just ground-up stale bread, right? What else is there to consider? Well, if you've recently tried what passes for breadcrumbs at the grocery store—overly milled, poorly spiced powders sold in cardboard tubes—you might realize there's a better option.

High-quality breadcrumbs are laughably easy to make at home and require only two things: stale bread and a little forethought. The breadcrumbs that result have real texture, hearty crunch, and a unique flavor. They can easily be adapted to fit your needs and preferences, from the type of bread you use to the addition of spices, salts, or dried herbs. This recipe—more of a method—is basic, and while it may seem a bit involved (as much as a recipe for breadcrumbs can be considered "involved"), it's reliable and won't disappoint.

First, you need old bread. We prefer using the leftovers of a rustic ciabatta, French, or sourdough loaf for a neutral flavor, but use what you have and be creative with your choice. For example, a good rye or pumpernickel makes for earthier breadcrumbs that pair well with Cheddar-based mac and cheeses. Avoid using bread that has dried fruits or nuts, as the moisture retained by the fruit may result in the crumbs becoming soft or moldy when you store them. If you've got bread with small seeds (poppy, sesame, etc.) or grains on the crust, feel free to use it, as these will lend intriguing flavor to your crumbs.

Whether you're using a whole loaf, a half a loaf, or a few slices, cut the bread into 1-inch cubes. Set them in a bowl and tuck them away somewhere in a dry cupboard and forget about them for a few days, but try not to forget-forget them. They should be stale but not hard as rocks. Place the dry cubes in a food processor, one cup at a time, as doing too much too quickly results in some of the cubes being blitzed to powder and others not getting chopped at all. Pulse a few times, add a pinch of good-quality sea salt and a crack of pepper, and pulse a few times more. You want the bread to break into coarse crumbs of various sizes, from large shards to tiny grains. You do not want to pulverize the bread into a fine powder.

That's it. You're done. Place the breadcrumbs in an airtight container and leave the top off overnight to get rid of any excess moisture before sealing it shut. They should taste perfectly fresh for about a month. If you'd like to give your crumbs a bit more personality, feel free to toss them with some dried herbs, ground spices, dried citrus zest, or grated hard cheese before using.

FRESH PANEER

IF YOU'VE EVER HAD INDIAN FOOD, YOU'VE LIKELY DISCOV-ered the fresh flavor and squeaky sound of paneer—a fresh cheese made throughout southern Asia. Since it's not made with rennet and doesn't melt, this cheese is a popular meat substitute for many vegetarians. The acid used to make paneer comes from yogurt, lemon juice, or vinegar, and the resulting soft but firm cheese stands up to frying, baking, and sautéing.

Paneer may not be as fancy as other artisan cheeses, but there are plenty of small producers who make paneer and sell it at local Indian markets and co-op grocery stores. Paneer, unlike most cheeses in this book, is usually available prepackaged in 8- to 16-ounce blocks. It is also incredibly easy to make at home, as it requires only milk, acid, cheesecloth, and a bit of patience. Making paneer is a simple project that can be done right before bed; you'll wake up the next day to fresh, homemade cheese, ready for cooking.

This recipe produces a straightforward paneer. Some like to add saffron, coriander, or other spices to the milk, and some even wrap their paneer in cilantro or basil for a bit of extra flavor. Play around with the recipe. Feel free to make your own artisan creation to eat on its own or to use in our paneer salad (page 35) or Indian-style mac and cheese (page 102).

HOMEMADE PANEER

MAKES ABOUT 6 TO 8 OUNCES OF PANEER

½   **gallon whole milk**

¼   **cup white vinegar**

Special equipment:
Cheesecloth

1.   In a heavy-bottomed pot, bring milk to a boil over medium-high heat. Slowly add the vinegar and stir. Keep stirring until curds have formed.

2.   Pour curds into a strainer lined with cheesecloth or a thin tea towel. Wrap up the curds tightly with the cloth and set in the sink. Place a cutting board weighed down with something heavy—like a hefty cookbook or a kettle filled with water—on top of the cheese to press out the remaining whey and bind the curds together. Allow to drain for 2 hours to overnight.

3.   Let the cheese set in the refrigerator for another hour before cutting it into cubes. At this point, you can use the paneer immediately or wrap it in plastic and store it in the refrigerator for up to three days.

CHAPTER 2:
ALWAYS REFRESHING

CHAPTER 2:
ALWAYS REFRESHING

The best

part of our weekends is when we're able to step outside of our busy schedules, turn off our phones and computers, and sit down to a simple lunch with friends. It doesn't have to be anything fancy. No silverware will be polished and the china will stay stacked in the cupboard. Instead, we'll throw down a sheet of linen over the picnic table, cut some flowers from the garden, and prepare simple, no-fuss fare. After all, who wants to waste those precious moments you could be spending with loved ones keeping track of four burners and wondering where the dessert forks went?

For us, lunch is a simple affair composed of whatever produce and cheeses are in season. (And, of course, whatever's in the fridge.) A touch of pasta can make a meal heartier, so guests leave feeling full and satisfied. When everyone gathers, we gab in the kitchen about this or that, one of us chopping a grassy wedge of Abbaye de Bel'loc while the other peels a sticky-sweet mango. Whoever is visiting gets to whisk together a vinaigrette or stir a bubbling pot of pasta. Food tastes so much better when everyone is involved in the preparation.

When lunch is served, the talking stops for a few minutes. The only sound is the occasional clinking of ice in mason jars filled with sweet tea, and the faint murmurs of "Mmmm . . ." These light cheese-and-pasta salads should be enjoyed in tranquillity and high spirits. They bring together a parade of colorful ingredients from every season and aim to please the senses and awaken the palate.

HUMBOLDT FOG WITH
GRILLED PEACHES AND ORZO

SERVES 4

3 freestone yellow peaches

2 tablespoons honey

2 tablespoons balsamic vinegar

2 tablespoons olive oil

   Sea salt

10 ounces orzo

¼ cup chopped parsley, plus more for garnish

¼ cup chopped spearmint

⅓ cup chopped pistachios

   Freshly ground black pepper

6 ounces Humboldt Fog, rind removed and cheese coarsely crumbled

WHAT COULD BE NICER THAN A BLUSHING PEACH? THE SUN-KISSED COLOR, THE TICKLISH feel of the fuzz, the sweet-as-sugarcane flavor. This simple orzo salad lets these traits shine—and without the nuisance of peach juice dribbling down your arm. Summer in a bowl, this is.

If there is any cheese that pairs best with a peach, it's Humboldt Fog. This humble yet multi-award-winning specimen was the herald for American-made artisan cheeses and shows up on nearly every cheese plate in the country, with good reason. Crafted by Cypress Grove in Humboldt County, California, this superlative goat cheese possesses plenty of flavor. Beneath this cheese's bloomy rind lies an intoxicating paste that guards its savory core: a line of decorative vegetable ash running through the middle, giving Humboldt Fog its distinct layer-cake appearance.

1. Using a barely damp paper towel, lightly scrub the peaches of any extraneous fuzz. Don't wash the peaches, as they will soak up excess water. Using a sharp knife, cut each peach in half lengthwise around the pit, using the peach's crevices as a guide. Discard the pits.

2. Set the peach halves in a zip-top bag and toss with honey, balsamic vinegar, olive oil, and a pinch of sea salt. Allow the peaches to marinate for 10 minutes.

3. While the peaches marinate, cook the orzo in some salted boiling water until al dente. Drain through a colander and set aside.

4. Once the peaches are done marinating, reserve the marinade and place the peach halves on a hot, oiled grill, cut-side down. Cover and cook for 5 to 8 minutes, or until the peaches are soft and have developed some charming dark grill marks. Roughly chop into bite-size pieces and set aside.

5. Combine the peaches, marinade, orzo, parsley, spearmint, and pistachios in a bowl and toss. Add a bit more sea salt and some freshly ground black pepper to taste. Plonk in the Humboldt Fog and toss once or twice, just enough to bring everything together. Overmixing will melt the cheese, and our goal here is to maintain its chunky texture.

ALTERNATIVE CHEESES: Though Humboldt Fog is widely available, a good stand-in would be Goat's Leap Eclipse, Bermuda Triangle, or any stellar chèvre.

WINE PAIRINGS: rosé, Sauvignon Blanc, Grüner Veltliner, Gewürztraminer

ADDITIONAL PAIRINGS FOR THE CHEESE: plums, cherries, balsamic vinegar reduction

BUFFALO MOZZARELLA
CAPRESE PASTA SALAD

SERVES 2 TO 4

- **8** ounces farfalle
- **8** ounces fresh buffalo mozzarella cheese, cut into ½-inch cubes
- **1** large handful fresh basil leaves, cut into chiffonade
- **3** large, tart heirloom tomatoes, chopped into ½-inch cubes
- **4** tablespoons extra-virgin olive oil

  Sea salt and freshly ground black pepper

  Balsamic vinegar

I REMEMBER HOT AFTERNOONS SPENT IN PUGLIA, IN SOUTHERN ITALY, WHERE FRESH mozzarella cheese is practically a staple. The people there are very proud of their fresh cheese, and dairymen regularly sell out of mozzarella before dinnertime. Often I had to elbow my way to the counter, battling diminutive—but exceptionally strong!—gray-haired Italian grandmothers so I wouldn't miss out on my favorite lunch: fresh mozzarella, a loaf of crusty bread, and a little *balsamico*.

Originating on the island of Capri, off the coast of southern Italy, *insalata caprese* is possibly the perfect warm-weather lunch. Tart heirloom tomatoes jazz up the smoothness of fresh *mozzarella di bufala*, an extra-tangy mozzarella made from buffalo milk. The addition of basil, with its pungent aroma, twirls the whole thing into a Mediterranean dream. Combined with pasta, this salad is a little more hearty than the standard caprese but still maintains its signature lightness. *Perfetto!* —SS

1. Cook the pasta in a large pot of salted boiling water until al dente. Drain through a colander for 5 minutes to completely dry the pasta. Toss the pasta a few times in the colander while it's draining to prevent sticking.

2. In a large bowl, toss pasta with cheese, basil, tomatoes, and olive oil. Season with salt and pepper, tossing until the salad ingredients are completely combined. Dish into small bowls and drizzle each bowl with a small amount of balsamic vinegar before serving.

ALTERNATIVE CHEESES: Any fresh mozzarella will do, though farm-made mozzarella is a treat that you'll never forget. We recommend you get the good stuff, which will shine in this dish.

WINE PAIRINGS: Sauvignon Blanc, Grechetto, Chablis, Roussette

ADDITIONAL PAIRINGS FOR THE CHEESE: balsamic vinegar reduction, extra-virgin olive oil, freshly ground black pepper, pomegranate

COW, SHEEP, AND GOAT MILK— WHAT'S THE DIFFERENCE?

CATTLE, SHEEP, AND GOATS ARE VERY different from one another, so it makes sense that they would produce very different kinds of milk. To the everyday cheese consumer, this means noticeable variances in the flavor and texture of the cheeses produced from each type of milk.

Cow's milk, for example, is relatively high in fat. As a general rule, cow's milk yields buttery cheeses with a grassy or beefy flavor. Think Brillat-Savarin, Roaring Forties Blue, and any good-quality Gruyère. Generally high in lactose, these cheeses can be tough for some people to digest, though harder cow's milk cheeses contain less lactose and are sometimes easier on the gut.

Goat's milk has a tangier, "goatier" flavor, which makes for much stronger-tasting cheeses. You'll notice a nice salty layer to fresh goat cheeses, which often have a gentle chalky texture. An aged goat cheese, such as Cypress Grove's Midnight Moon, Vermont Creamery's Bonne Bouche, or any goat's-milk Gouda, will have a more assertive personality than its bovine-sourced equivalents. For some, goat cheeses are easier to digest than those made from cow's milk, due to goat's milk's unique protein structure.

Sheep's milk has quite a bit more fat than cow's milk, which makes sheep's-milk cheeses incredibly rich and satisfying. In fact, taste a piece and you'll notice the oil from the fat on your tongue. This kind of milk imparts a sweet, grassy, nutty flavor to cheeses, and when used in hard varieties of cheeses, sheep's milk can produce caramelly flavor notes that knock every other cheese out of the park. For the best examples of sheep's-milk cheese, hunt down Ewephoria sheep's-milk Gouda, a stout Pecorino, or your local cheese-monger's favorite Manchego.

Want the best of all worlds? Try a mixed-milk cheese that blends two or three different milks. A few of our favorites:

- LA TUR—cow, sheep, and goat
- CAMPO DE MONTALBAN—cow, sheep, and goat
- BLEATING HEART'S MIXTRESS—cow and sheep
- VERMONT CREAMERY'S CREMONT—cow and goat
- ACHADINHA CHEESE COMPANY'S BRONCHA— cow and goat

And if you ever happen across cheeses made from the milk of buffalo, yak, or camel, we highly recommend you give them a try. These milks have entirely unique flavor qualities that you won't find anywhere else.

DRUNKEN GOAT WITH
EDAMAME, FENNEL, AND ROTINI

SERVES 4

10 ounces rotini

10 ounces Drunken Goat, rind intact, cut into 1-inch cubes

5 tablespoons lemon juice

1 cup fresh-shelled edamame beans

¼ pound fennel bulb, sliced paper thin (about 1½ cups sliced)

4 tablespoons fresh mint leaves, cut into chiffonade

3 tablespoons chopped fennel fronds

3 tablespoons extra-virgin olive oil

Zest of 1 medium lemon

Sea salt

Freshly ground black pepper

I WAS WARY THE FIRST TIME MY LOCAL CHEESEMONGER COAXED ME INTO TRYING Drunken Goat. In his description, this semifirm goat variety sounded like the frat boy of fine cheese: boozy, hotheaded, and likely to disappoint. How wrong I was! Grassy and fresh, with the aroma of wet clover and a hint of zing from the Spanish red wine it is bathed in, Drunken Goat is not fratty at all. Rather, it's like the sleek, sexy track star I fell in love with in college.

This is a cheese that shouldn't be burdened with a heavy sauce or lots of cream—a light dressing of lemon and oil is all it needs, with edamame, mint, and fennel complementing the greener flavors of the cheese. If you're looking to impress at your next outdoor potluck or picnic, this beautiful dish will do it.   —SS

1. Cook the pasta in salted boiling water until al dente. Drain through a colander and wash with cold water to cool. Drain the excess water.

2. Toss all the ingredients together in a bowl. Taste the salad. If you feel it needs more lemon, herbs, salt, or pepper, then adjust and taste again. When it's balanced to your satisfaction, serve and be amazed at how easy that was.

ALTERNATIVE CHEESES: Lamb Chopper, Midnight Moon

WINE PAIRINGS: Sauvignon Blanc, dry Riesling, Grüner Veltliner

ADDITIONAL PAIRINGS FOR THE CHEESE: edamame, honey, dates, fig jam

BAKED CAMEMBERT
WITH PEARS AND SHELL PASTA

SERVES 2

1 (8-ounce) wheel of Camembert

1 tablespoon maple syrup

4 tips of fresh rosemary or 2 small whole sprigs

6 ounces small shell pasta

1 Anjou, Bosc, or Comice pear, cored and sliced thin

½ cup raisins

1 tablespoon olive oil

Freshly ground black pepper

ALTERNATIVE CHEESES: Bent River Camembert, Rouge et Noir Yellow Buck Camembert, Brie, Camellia

WINE PAIRINGS: Sparkling Chenin Blanc, champagne, sparkling rosé

ADDITIONAL PAIRINGS FOR THE CHEESE: pears, sautéed mushrooms, mushroom pâté, white truffles

AUTHENTIC CAMEMBERT IS UNAVAILABLE IN THE UNITED STATES DUE TO THE AOC standards (*appellation d'origine contrôlée*, or name-protected) by which it is produced. It's made with unpasteurized milk and it is aged for less than sixty days—huge no-no's by American food-safety laws. If you want true Camembert, you'll need to have a friend smuggle it into the States or get your fill while visiting France.

Luckily, you can buy Hervé Mons's Camembert at many large-scale gourmet groceries. Mons, a professional *affineur* (a specialist in aging cheese), sought to provide a pasteurized Camembert that was similar to AOC Camembert. This proud example boasts a robust country flavor with a slight garlic scent.

We enjoy baked Camembert; when we were kids, back in the 1980s, we'd secretly watch our parents make it for themselves after we'd been sent to bed. They would cover it in honey and herbs, bake it, cut off the top, and serve it as a dip with veggies and crusty bread. This recipe uses a similar approach. Like a retro fondue, the baked cheese is spooned over a simple meal of pasta and pears. Feel free to simply smear the cheese over bits of toast as well.

1. Boil a large pot of lightly salted water on the stovetop. Preheat oven to 350°F. Take the Camembert out of its wooden box (if it came in one, which it usually does) and remove the wax paper. Place a 10-inch-square piece of foil in the box and replace the Camembert. Score the top of the Camembert with a knife and drizzle with maple syrup. Poke the rosemary tips or sprigs into the scored sections and bake for 30 minutes. (Don't worry, the box will not scorch if you stick to our time and temperature recommendations.) The cheese will be oozy and tempting.

2. During the last 10 minutes of the cheese's baking time, cook the pasta in the boiling water until al dente. Drain through a colander. Toss pasta with the pears, raisins, olive oil, and pepper. Divide between two plates.

3. Once the cheese is finished, cut open the top, spoon the gooey insides over the pasta, and serve immediately. If the cheese sets up too quickly, pop it back in the oven; if it cools down too much before you serve it, place dishes under the broiler for a minute or two.

Another option is to serve it like fondue, dipping forkfuls of pasta and fruit into the hot pool of cheese. It's a little messy, but a lot more fun.

Note: *Be sure that the box is held together with staples and not glue, as glued boxes tend to come undone in a hot oven. If the box is glued or there was no box, bake the Camembert in an aluminum-foil-lined ramekin or other small ceramic baking dish.*

PANEER, PINEAPPLE,
AND CUCUMBER PASTA SALAD

SERVES 4

- **4** ounces spiral pasta such as rotini, fusilli, or gemelli
- **1½** tablespoons olive oil, divided
- **2** cups cubed paneer (for recipe, see page 23)
  - Sea salt
  - Freshly ground black pepper
- **1** cucumber, peeled, seeded, and sliced
- **3** cups chopped pineapple
- **¼** cup cilantro, roughly chopped
  - Juice of 2 limes
  - Zest of 2 limes
  - Pinch of cayenne pepper

THE MILKY FLAVOR OF PANEER IS TASTY, BUT WHEN THE CHEESE IS LIGHTLY SAUTÉED in oil, the sugars and fats in it caramelize to make paneer even more delectable. Heating allows you to better taste the origins of the cheese, the grassy meadows where the cows grazed before giving up their milk. Cooking also crisps up parts of the cheese, giving them a toasted, wheaty flavor and firmer texture. You'll realize the paneer is just as excited about all this as you are when you bite into it and it meets your teeth with a cheerful squeak of appreciation.

This salad takes lightly sautéed paneer and combines it with pineapple, cool cucumber, and jubilant twirls of pasta. It's a simple and impressive pasta salad, very different from most others you'll taste at your average picnic.

1. Cook the pasta in a large pot of salted boiling water until al dente. Drain through a colander and rinse with cool water to stop the cooking process. Drain again and set aside.

2. Place 1 tablespoon olive oil in a sauté pan over medium-high heat. Add the paneer, lightly salt and pepper it, and sauté until the cheese takes on a light golden crust on all sides.

3. Toss the paneer in a bowl with the pasta, cucumber, pineapple, and cilantro. In another small bowl, whisk together the lime juice, zest, cayenne pepper, and remaining olive oil. Toss the dressing with the salad. Taste and adjust seasoning as desired. Serve.

ALTERNATIVE CHEESES: haloumi, queso fresco

WINE PAIRINGS: Verdejo, Torrontés, rosé, Sauvignon Blanc

ADDITIONAL PAIRINGS FOR THE CHEESE: mint, curry, tropical fruits, lamb, goat, cilantro, cooked tomatoes

PASTA SALAD WITH DOLCELATTE
AND CONCORD GRAPES

8 ounces spiral pasta, such as fusilli

1½ cups walnut halves, coarsely chopped

½ cup olive oil

5 tablespoons red wine vinegar

2 tablespoons honey

½ cup minced shallots (1 whole bulb)

Sea salt

Freshly ground black pepper

2 cups Concord grapes, halved and seeded

6 ounces Dolcelatte, broken into small crumbles

WE KNOW—NOT EVERYONE LIKES BLUE CHEESE. IT SEEMS THAT SOME PEOPLE DON'T find the idea of eating spoiled milk riddled with mold appetizing. Those who do deign to try it may be frightened away, possibly permanently, by the fiery spice of the more bludgeoning blues.

So it's best to start off blue-cheese newbies with something soft, sweet, and simple. Dolcelatte (sometimes called Gorgonzola Dolce) is a perfect starter cheese for the blue-cheese-phobic. It isn't true Italian Gorgonzola, which is aged longer and thus possesses a much punchier flavor, but it has a similar taste and mouthfeel. The milk in this cheese is sweeter and the mold not as forward, making it a perfect beginner's blue, and the cheese is offset by the sweetness of fresh grapes. This simple salad could convert even the most recalcitrant hater to the way of the blue.

1. Cook the pasta in a large pot of salted boiling water until al dente. Drain through a colander and rinse with cool water to stop the cooking process. Drain again and set aside.

2. Place the walnuts in a nonstick pan and roast over medium heat until they are fragrant and lightly toasted. Remove from heat.

3. Place the oil, vinegar, honey, and shallots in a bowl and whisk until combined. Check the flavor, and add salt and pepper to taste. Set aside the vinaigrette.

4. Toss pasta, walnuts, grapes, and cheese together in a bowl. Gently fold in vinaigrette. Cover with plastic wrap and allow the flavors to marinate for at least an hour, or serve immediately if you just can't stand to wait.

Note: *Concord grapes, even when in season, aren't always available. Feel free to substitute any black or red table grape, though the winey flavor of Concords is preferred for this recipe.*

ALTERNATIVE CHEESES: Cashel Blue, Fourme d'Ambert, Gorgonzola, Stilton

WINE PAIRINGS: sweeter Chenin Blancs, sweet Riesling, unoaked gently sweet whites

ADDITIONAL PAIRINGS FOR THE CHEESE: pears, grapes, apple compote, pecans

THE CHEESE HAS EYES

GROWING UP, YOU MAY HAVE WONDERED why the Swiss cheese slices your mom put on your lunchtime sandwich had holes in them. Perhaps a mouse got to the cheese first? Or maybe the Swiss are just stingy with their cheese?

The reason, as with many interesting cheese-related phenomena, is bacteria. *Propionibacterium freudenreichii* is a bacterium that consumes lactic acid and, in the process, releases carbon dioxide as well as other by-products. These little bubbles of CO_2 collect in small fissures between the curds and expand into large bubbles, called eyes. This chemical reaction is also what gives the cheese its characteristic nutty flavor.

The most widely known holey cheese is Emmentaler, which we in the United States refer to as Swiss cheese. There is, in fact, no individual cheese that is officially called Swiss cheese; there are instead many varieties of Swiss cheeses, which are also known as Alpine cheeses. Other excellent holey cheeses include Flösserkäse, Raclette, and Prättigauer.

Today, these holes are relished, though they were once seen as imperfections. Large gaping holes indicate a cheese that's been well aged and has depth of flavor. It's worth noting, though, that in the United States, the USDA has regulations on the size of the holes: they have to be from ⅜ to ¹³⁄₁₆ of an inch in diameter, so that machines can cut the cheese into uniform slices. Larger holes, apparently, result in torn cheese slices. Uniformity has its price—in this instance, Swiss cheesemakers are forced to export cheeses that aren't as delectable as they could be without such restrictions.

RADICCHIO, MANGO, AND
MOZZARELLA SALAD WITH CAVATAPPI

SERVES 2 TO 4

- **10** ounces cavatappi
- **2** large mangoes, peeled, seeded, and chopped into ½-inch cubes
- **8** large radicchio leaves, thick base parts removed, chopped coarsely
- **½** small sweet red onion, cut in half and sliced thinly
- **1** pound fresh mozzarella, cut into ½-inch cubes
- **¼** cup freshly squeezed orange juice
- **1** tablespoon orange zest
  Juice of half a lime
- **¼** cup extra-virgin olive oil
- **2** tablespoons balsamic vinegar
  Sea salt
  Freshly ground white pepper
- **⅓** cup cilantro leaves, coarsely chopped, for garnish

THERE ARE FEW THINGS WE LOVE MORE THAN A BALL OF FRESHLY MADE MOZZARELLA. In Italy, mozzarella-making is a family affair, with sons following their fathers into the dairy world. Techniques are taught, cattle bloodlines are handed down, and traditions are cemented through countless generations. You can always tell a mozzarella-cheese man by his hands: they are permanently pink with the scars of handling scalding-hot curds, which must be stretched by hand to get the proper texture.

This salad, which packs a strong zing of citrus, is perfect for those days when you're looking for a light and refreshing lunch that will nonetheless carry you through an afternoon of activity. The bitter snap of radicchio is courted aggressively by the accompanying sweet-tart orange vinaigrette, while a touch of onion brings just a lick of heat to the dish.

1. Cook the pasta in a large pot of salted boiling water until al dente. Drain through a colander and rinse with cool water to stop the cooking process. Allow to drain through the colander for 5 minutes to completely dry the pasta, tossing occasionally.

2. In a large bowl, toss pasta with mangoes, radicchio, red onions, and mozzarella until everything is completely combined.

3. In a small bowl, whisk together orange juice, orange zest, lime juice, olive oil, and balsamic vinegar until combined. Use a steady, even beating pattern to make sure your emulsion forms. Once the vinaigrette comes together, season to taste with salt and a generous amount of white pepper.

4. Drizzle the salad with vinaigrette and toss so that all radicchio leaves and pasta are coated evenly—you may not need all the dressing. Dish into small bowls and serve sprinkled with chopped cilantro.

ALTERNATIVE CHEESES: Any fresh mozzarella will do, though farm-made mozzarella is a treat that you'll never forget. When we say *fresh mozzarella*, we mean the stuff that comes in a tub of water, not the dry stuff that resembles a softball. Spring for good mozzarella—you won't regret it.

WINE PAIRINGS: Roero Arneis, Prosecco, Barbera, Dolcetto Grechetto, Sauvignon Blanc

ADDITIONAL PAIRINGS FOR THE CHEESE: extra-virgin olive oil, white pepper, pomegranate, fresh basil, heirloom tomatoes

YODELING GOAT WITH
GOLDEN BEETS AND ORECCHIETTE

SERVES 4 TO 6

For the vinaigrette:

- 2 **Meyer lemons**
- 2 **teaspoons sugar, divided**
- 1½ **teaspoons chopped fresh tarragon**
- ½ **teaspoon lemon zest**
- ½ **teaspoon sea salt**
- ¼ **teaspoon freshly ground black pepper**
- ½ **cup high-quality, fruity olive oil**
- 1 **tablespoon heavy cream**

For the salad:

- 6 **medium golden beets, peeled and cut into ½-inch cubes (substitute regular beets if need be)**
- 2 **tablespoons olive oil**
- 1 **cup whole almonds, skin on**
- 10 **ounces orecchiette**
- 1 **pound Yodeling Goat, rind removed, shredded**
- ½ **cup caramelized Meyer lemon vinaigrette**

FLORAL, SWEET, AND RICH, YODELING GOAT IS A LOVELY CHEESE THAT IMPARTS JUST a hint of its former goaty life. You'll find only a touch of salty sharpness on the palate; its most noticeable quality is a buttery texture that tames most of the capriciousness that goat's milk often displays. If you're looking for a cheese to help convert goat-cheese skeptics, Yodeling Goat may be your best bet.

This refreshing, early-spring dream of a salad is a colorful sight to behold: canary-yellow beets, a touch of tarragon, and a caramelized Meyer lemon vinaigrette provide brightness in both the visual and culinary senses. You'll want to make the vinaigrette first so you can dress the salad as soon as it's ready.

To make the vinaigrette:

1. Cut lemons in half. Sprinkle some of the sugar on the cut surface of each lemon half—the exposed lemon should be fully coated with sugar. Reserve the remaining sugar for the dressing. Heat a small frying pan over medium heat and press the sugared side of each lemon half to the surface of the pan. Let cook for 2 to 3 minutes, enough for the lemons to brown but not burn. Occasionally apply gentle pressure to them while cooking to improve surface contact. The fruit should become lemony-fragrant. Remove lemons from pan and allow to cool. Once they're cool, squeeze the juice from the lemons into a bowl, measure out 3 tablespoons for the dressing, and do what you like with the rest. Remove any seeds from the juice.

2. Combine 3 tablespoons lemon juice, tarragon, lemon zest, salt, pepper, and remaining sugar in a bowl. Whisk quickly until well mixed. Slowly add a few table-spoons of olive oil and whisk quickly until the emulsion builds. Slowly drizzle in the remaining oil, then the cream, all the while whisking quickly and evenly. Add more sugar, salt, and pepper to taste. Pour over salad and serve immediately.

To make the salad:

1. Preheat the oven to 350°F. Place beets into a 9-by-9-inch glass baking dish and toss with olive oil. Roast for 55 to 60 minutes. Remove from oven and allow to cool.

2. While beets are cooking, heat a skillet over a medium flame and roast almonds until they are fragrant and just beginning to brown, about 4 minutes. Toss occasionally while cooking to allow for even browning. Remove almonds from heat and allow to cool. Once they are cool, chop coarsely so they are roughly ¼ to ½ their normal size.

3. Cook the pasta in a large pot of salted boiling water until al dente. Drain through a colander and rinse with cool water to stop the cooking process. Drain thoroughly and toss vigorously in a strainer to get rid of excess water hiding in the pasta's bowl-shaped divots. » recipe continues

4. Toss pasta, beets, almonds, and cheese in a bowl and then portion. Lightly drizzle with vinaigrette. Serve immediately.

ALTERNATIVE CHEESES: Midnight Moon, Tumalo Farms Classico, any flavorful goat Gouda

WINE PAIRINGS: Sauvignon Blanc, unoaked Chardonnay, Roero Arneis from Piedmont, Pinot Noir, vin gris, Syrah rosés

ADDITIONAL PAIRINGS FOR THE CHEESE: lemon chutney, lemon marmalade, fresh fennel, dried fennel seeds, fenugreek

CHOCOLATE PASTA

THE FIRST TIME WE HEARD ABOUT CHOCOlate pasta, our hearts immediately leaped with the image of rich, cocoa-colored noodles smothered with ice cream and caramel sauce. That vision was shattered with the first nibble, though, as traditional chocolate pasta is very much *not* meant to be lumped into the dessert category.

While this type of pasta does indeed taste of chocolate, some varieties take liberties by sharing cocoa's more savory flavor qualities; instead of the expected sugary impact, the noodles can be bitter, earthy, and occasionally astringent, depending on the brand.

For some, chocolate pasta is an acquired taste, but pair it with prosciutto, a light cream sauce, and a touch of crushed red pepper, and you'll become an instant convert. Or see our recipe pairing it with Bucherondin on page 44 for our favorite recipe.

ASPARAGUS SALAD WITH RICOTTA
SALATA, FAVA BEANS, MINT, AND FARFALLE

SERVES 4 TO 6

- 1 cup shelled fava beans (1 pound in the pod)
- 10 ounces farfalle
- 1 pound asparagus, woody ends broken off, cut diagonally into 1-inch sticks
- 3 tablespoons avocado oil, divided (substitute olive oil if you wish)

  Sea salt

  Freshly ground black pepper
- 8 ounces ricotta salata, broken into small chunks
- ¼ cup mint leaves, cut into chiffonade

  Juice and zest of 1 lime

THIS BRIGHT SPRING SALAD IS PERFECT FOR AN IMPROMPTU RAINY DAY LUNCH PARTY. It comes together quickly and celebrates the greenest bounty the season has to offer. It has become one of our go-to meals during April and May, when pencil-thin asparagus stand at attention and the mint in our gardens begins its Napoleonic advance on every bit of available space. Add the lime and you've got a lovely Mojito-like pasta salad.

Ricotta salata is ricotta cheese that's been pressed and salted, resulting in a firmer—though not at all heavy—cheese. Deep green avocado oil adds a smooth flavor to the asparagus and fava beans. The asparagus is cooked in a skillet, but if you have a grill, try roasting the asparagus over the flames to kiss it with a bit of pungent smoke.

1. Bring a large pot of water to a boil. Add 2 teaspoons salt and bring back to a boil. Blanch the fava beans for about 1 minute. You'll know they're done when they begin to float. Scoop the beans out with a slotted spoon and rinse under cold water. When they are cool enough to handle, carefully slip them out of their little jackets. Set the beans aside and discard the jackets. Do not discard the water.

2. In the same water you used for the fava beans, cook the pasta until it is al dente. Drain through a colander and set aside.

3. Heat 1 tablespoon of avocado oil in a sauté pan over medium-high heat. When the oil is hot and shimmering, add the asparagus and sprinkle with salt and pepper. Cook until the asparagus has blistered a bit, about 4 minutes, flipping occasionally. Do not overcook the asparagus or it will get too soft.

4. Toss the fava beans, pasta, asparagus, ricotta salata, mint, lime juice, and lime zest together in a large bowl. Salt and pepper to taste. Drizzle with the remaining avocado oil and serve.

ALTERNATIVE CHEESES: feta, haloumi, paneer, queso fresco

WINE PAIRINGS: Sauvignon Blanc, Muscadet (Melon de Bourgogne), Grüner Veltliner

ADDITIONAL PAIRINGS FOR THE CHEESE: English snap peas, fennel, pine nuts, thyme, mint

CHOCOLATE PASTA WITH
BUCHERONDIN, HAZELNUTS, AND CHERRIES

SERVES 2 TO 4

- ¼ cup plus 2 tablespoons hazelnut oil
- 2 tablespoons red wine vinegar
- 2 tablespoons maple syrup
- ¼ teaspoon mustard powder
- 1 heaping tablespoon cocoa nibs
- Pinch of sea salt
- Pinch of freshly ground black pepper
- ½ cup hazelnuts
- 12 ounces chocolate pasta (preferably linguine, but use what you can find)
- 5 ounces Bucherondin, roughly broken apart
- 1 cup pitted cherries (Bing, Brooks, or Rainier are all lovely varieties)
- 2 cups whole arugula leaves, washed and dried

YOU NEED AT LEAST ONE SUPERBLY ESOTERIC RECIPE IN YOUR REPERTOIRE, SOMETHING easy to put together using one or two chic ingredients that will take your culinary reputation up a peg and make you a champion in the kitchen. This is that dish. Bitter chocolate pasta, whole cherries, toasted hazelnuts, and a hazelnut–cocoa nib vinaigrette conspire to produce a savory treat that will amaze your guests.

All this comes together around a Loire cheese called Bucherondin. Bucherondin sounds like the name of a French superhero; taste this lovely goat cheese, and you may very well decide that's exactly what it is. Smooth and chalky at first, it sheds its mild-mannered identity and reveals an astonishing tang and spice.

1. Preheat the oven to 350°F. Place the hazelnut oil, red wine vinegar, maple syrup, mustard powder, cocoa nibs, salt, and pepper in a jar with a tight-fitting lid and shake vigorously to combine. (A bowl and whisk will do this job just fine too.) Taste and adjust seasonings as desired. Set aside.

2. Place the hazelnuts on a baking sheet and toast in the oven for 10 to 15 minutes, or until the skins darken and blister, and the nuts are hauntingly fragrant. Wrap the hazelnuts in a clean dishtowel and leave them to steam for 1 minute. Rub the nuts in the dishtowel to scrub the skins off. Don't worry if some of the skins stay; you just want the bulk of them removed. Roughly chop the nuts and set aside.

3. While the hazelnuts are roasting, cook the pasta until al dente. Drain through a colander and divide the pasta evenly among bowls.

4. Scatter the Bucherondin over the top of the pasta, followed by the cherries and hazelnuts. Top each bowl joyfully with a carefree handful of arugula, dress with the vinaigrette, and serve.

ALTERNATIVE CHEESES: Bûcheron, Zingerman's Lincoln Log, Caña de Cabra

WINE PAIRINGS: rosés, California Pinot Noirs

ADDITIONAL PAIRINGS FOR THE CHEESE: preserved cherries, tea preserves, fresh figs, mangoes

YOGURT CHICKEN SALAD
WITH ABBAYE DE BEL'LOC AND FUSILLI

SERVES 6

- 10 ounces fusilli
- ½ cup slivered almonds
- 1 cup whole-milk yogurt
- 1½ tablespoons curry powder
- 1¼ tablespoons honey
- 1 tablespoon lemon juice

  Zest of 1 medium lemon

  Pinch of salt

  Freshly ground black pepper

- 2 cups cooked chicken, shredded
- 6 ounces Abbaye de Bel'loc, cut into ½-inch cubes
- 3 green onions, thinly sliced
- ¾ cup roughly chopped dried apricots, packed tightly
- 1 apple, peeled, cored, and chopped

DON'T GET ME WRONG: A MAYO-SAUCED CHICKEN SALAD IS NOT ONLY DELICIOUSLY retro but tasty too. Still, once in a while, a chicken salad with yogurt can be a welcome change. It's lighter, tangier, and more refreshing. Oh, and healthy too. So there's that if you're into it.

This chicken salad is fragrant with lemon, curry powder, and honey, the way my grandmother in Ojai, California, always made it. She'd often toss in some almonds and dried apricots, both harvested from her own yard or from the trees of her neighbors. The addition of Abbaye de Bel'loc, a French cheese made by monks at the eponymous abbey, adds a nice salty, grassy twang to the salad. It's a great way to use the leftovers from the previous night's roast chicken. —GM

1. Cook the pasta in a large pot of salted boiling water until al dente. Drain through a colander and set aside.

2. Toast the almonds in a dry skillet over medium heat until golden and fragrant. Set aside.

3. Whisk together the yogurt, curry powder, honey, lemon juice, lemon zest, salt, and pepper. Taste and adjust seasoning as desired.

4. When the pasta is cool to the touch, toss it in a large bowl with the chicken, cheese, green onions, apricots, apple, almonds, and yogurt sauce. Serve.

ALTERNATIVE CHEESES: Carr Valley Benedictine, Hidden Springs Creamery Ocooch Mountain, Gabietou, Shepherd's Way Farms Friesago

WINE PAIRINGS: Gewürztraminer, Tocai Friulano, Grüner Veltliner

ADDITIONAL PAIRINGS FOR THE CHEESE: fresh figs, dried figs, quince, prunes

BLUE HEAVEN

RECENTLY WE SAT STONY-FACED AND AMBIV-alent as cheese after cheese made its way over the counter at our regular cheese shop. One tasted like cardboard. Another was vaguely reminiscent of packing peanuts. Yet a third, with the promise of raw, goaty throatiness, delivered nothing at all beyond the blank taste of dental wax.

Finally, a slip of paper containing two slices of crumbly blue appeared from behind the counter. After so much disappointment, we warily eyeballed the cheesemonger, who nodded earnestly at the sheet of parchment. "No, really," he chirped nervously. "I think you'll like this one."

With a sigh, we nibbled; a second later, we smiled. Snappy to the nose and silky to the tongue, this blue wasn't flat or indistinct—it was alive, humming on our palates like a happy house cat sitting in front of a wood-burning stove.*

This is why we love blue cheese. It rarely fails to impress.

For those uninitiated into the Sacred Order of the Blue, these heady cheeses are worth learning to love. At first they may come off as abrasive, creating a physical spark of sensation on the tongue, but their vivacity imparts a flavor experience that you won't find anywhere else. If you're still unsure but interested in learning more, here are a few introductory varieties to guide you into the world of blue cheese:

- **BAYLEY HAZEN BLUE**

- **CASHEL**

- **FOURME D'AMBERT**

- **HIDDEN SPRINGS BOHEMIAN BLUE**

- **DUNBARTON BLUE** (a Cheddar-blue hybrid, for those who really need to ease into going blue)

In case you were wondering, this particular cheese was Roaring Forties blue, which you can find on page 62. It's a strong, abrasive specimen ready for any seasoned blue-cheese challenger.

CLASSIC BLUE LOG WITH ROASTED
RHUBARB, ROSEMARY WALNUTS, AND ROTINI

SERVES 4

- 1½ cups chopped walnuts
- ¼ cup plus 2 teaspoons olive oil, divided
- 1 tablespoon freshly minced rosemary leaves
- Pinch of cayenne pepper
- Pinch of sea salt
- Pinch of freshly ground black pepper
- 2 cups chopped rhubarb, in ½-inch pieces
- 2 tablespoons sugar
- 1 tablespoon honey
- Zest of 1 medium lemon
- Zest of 1 medium orange
- 6 ounces rotini
- ½ cup plus 1 tablespoon balsamic vinegar
- 4 cups arugula
- 1 (4.5-ounce) Classic Blue Log, quartered lengthwise and chopped into ½-inch pieces

ALTERNATIVE CHEESES: Montenebro, White Buck, Hubbardston Blue, Valençay, Laura Chenel Chèvre, Purple Haze, Leonora

WINE PAIRINGS: off-dry Chenin Blanc, Riesling, Syrah, sparkling rosé

ADDITIONAL PAIRINGS FOR THE CHEESE: Fuyu persimmons, pomegranates, cherry preserves

RHUBARB IS BY FAR ONE OF OUR FAVORITE FLAVORS, WHICH MAY SEEM ODD SINCE IT is often described as grippingly astringent and unpalatable. When raw, it can indeed be abrasive, but toss it with a bit of sugar, bake it in cream, cook it down into jam, or serve it with berries, and the blush of floral flavors is released. Submit rhubarb to any number of preparations, and it brings to mind April rains and the shedding of heavy cold-weather jackets.

One of rhubarb's lesser-known flavor mates is rosemary. Their culinary tryst is one that nobody seems to know about, except rhubarb's and rosemary's closest friends. This salad brings their relationship out into the open and joins them with yet a third partner, the inimitably tangy Classic Blue Log.

Classic Blue Log is a gem of a cheese that's striking in appearance and captivating in flavor. Produced by the Stetson family at Westfield Farm in Massachusetts, this goat's-milk cheese is enveloped in a velvety blue-gray mold. Don't let the fuzzy exterior scare you; inside is a cheese that's creamy, smooth, and reminiscent of wet stone with a hint of pine.

1. Preheat oven to 325°F. In a bowl, toss together the walnuts with 1½ tablespoons of the olive oil, rosemary, cayenne pepper, salt, and pepper. Spread walnuts on a baking sheet lined with aluminum foil and bake for 17 to 20 minutes, until the nuts are toasted and fragrant. Set aside to cool and turn oven up to 400°F. While the walnuts are toasting, prepare the rhubarb.

2. Toss the rhubarb, sugar, honey, and zests together in a bowl and let sit for 10 minutes to macerate. Spread the sweetened rhubarb in a single layer on a rimmed baking sheet and roast for 6 to 8 minutes. The rhubarb should still be crisp but no longer stringy; toothsome with a bit of give. If it still tastes sour, sprinkle with a little more sugar and roast for another few minutes. Set aside and reserve the juices in the pan, as these will be used for the dressing. Cool to room temperature.

3. Cook the pasta in a large pot of salted boiling water until al dente. Drain through a colander and set aside.

4. While the pasta cooks, make the dressing. Whisk together the remaining olive oil, the balsamic vinegar, and 3 tablespoons of the juices from the pan the rhubarb was roasted in.

5. Toss the arugula, pasta, walnuts, rhubarb, and Classic Blue Log together with the dressing. Serve.

SUMMER PASTA SALAD
WITH FRUIT SALSA

SERVES 4

8   ounces elbow macaroni

¼   cup chopped onion

1   cup pineapple chunks

1   cup chopped mango

½   cup chopped yellow peaches, skin on

½   cup chopped strawberries

½   jalapeño pepper, seeds removed, chopped

1   tablespoon lemon zest

2   tablespoons lemon juice

¼   cup chopped mint

1   teaspoon sea salt

3   tablespoons pineapple juice

¾   pound queso fresco, crumbled

    Additional lemon juice and sea salt for garnish

QUESO FRESCO—SPANISH FOR "FRESH CHEESE"—IS THE KIND OF WONDERFULLY LIGHT cheese you can eat a ton of without tiring of it, even on the hottest of days. Salty, bright, and tasting of fresh milk, this cheese is a perfect snack for a sweltering afternoon.

Paired with a sweet-tart summer fruit salsa, queso fresco's signature soft personality is highlighted by a generous amount of fruity acid. This cheese has a lighter flavor, though some varieties are saltier than others. If you feel that your cheese is on the saltier side of the spectrum, reduce the amount of salt in this dish by half. You may also find this cheese under the name queso blanco.

1. Cook the pasta in a large pot of salted boiling water until al dente. Drain through a colander and rinse with cool water to stop the cooking process. Drain again and set aside.

2. While the pasta is cooking, add onion, pineapple, mango, peaches, strawberries, jalapeño, lemon zest, lemon juice, mint, and sea salt to the bowl of a food processor. Pulse 3 times to get a nice, chunky consistency, but don't pulverize it into a puree. The goal is big chunks that are coarsely chopped.

3. Pour the salsa into a large bowl. Add pineapple juice 1 tablespoon at a time until desired sweetness is achieved. Add another squirt or two of lemon juice to taste. Fold in cheese and pasta. Serve topped with a sprinkling of sea salt.

ALTERNATIVE CHEESES: paneer or other mild, salty, milky, fresh cheese

WINE PAIRINGS: off-dry Riesling, sparkling dry or off-dry Chenin Blanc or Riesling, sparkling or still rosé

ADDITIONAL PAIRINGS FOR THE CHEESE: dried chili peppers, almonds, roast pork, dark chocolate

CHEF'S SALAD WITH ROTINI,
OSSAU-IRATY, AND SEARED
DUCK BREAST

SERVES 4 TO 6

- **8 ounces rotini**
- **¼ cup red wine vinegar**
- **2 tablespoons orange marmalade**
- **1 tablespoon Dijon mustard**
- **½ cup plus 1 teaspoon olive oil, divided**
- **Sea salt**
- **Freshly ground black pepper**
- **1 to 2 duck breasts, with skin (about 1 pound total, depending on the breed of duck)**
- **¼ pound mixed greens**
- **6 ounces Ossau-Iraty, cut into ½-inch cubes**
- **2 Roma tomatoes, seeded and cut into slices**

This chef's salad is built to feature Ossau-Iraty Brebis-Pyrénées (often simply called Ossau-Iraty), a Basque-style cheese made with sheep's milk. The name Ossau-Iraty refers to a large family of cheeses made in the area near the Ossau River. The cheese is olivey, fruity, and reminiscent of hazelnuts.

Duck's succulence and crispy skin give a royal boost to this cheese's complex, nutty flavors. The vinaigrette is inspired by *mostarda*, an Italian condiment of fruit tossed with mustard oil, and provides a reverberating tang, a bitterness, and a muted sweetness to placate the fattier, assertive flavors of the salad. We recommend serving this salad whenever you want to one-up a friend who fancies himself or herself a salad-making master; a gentle yet effective culinary smackdown if there ever was one.

1. Cook the pasta in a large pot of salted boiling water until al dente. Drain through a colander and rinse with cold water to cool noodles and stop the cooking process. Drain again and set aside.

2. Whisk together the red wine vinegar, marmalade, Dijon mustard, and ½ cup olive oil in a bowl. Salt and pepper to taste. Set aside.

3. Score the skin side of the duck in a crosshatch pattern, making sure not to cut into the meat. Lightly oil a skillet with 1 teaspoon of olive oil. Place the duck in the skillet, skin side down, and turn the heat to medium-high. You want to start with a cold pan, as it will render the fat and crisp the skin better than starting with a hot pan. Once the duck begins to sizzle, turn the heat down to medium and cook for 6 to 8 minutes to render the fat and crisp the skin. Flip the breast and cook the other side for 3 minutes. Do not overcook or the duck will become very tough. Remove from pan and loosely cover the duck with a foil tent. Allow the duck to rest for 5 minutes before slicing into ⅛- to ¼-inch slices. The rendered fat can be saved in a covered jar in the fridge and used within a week. (Fry some thinly sliced potatoes in it for a decadent side dish.)

4. Toss the pasta and greens in a bowl with the vinaigrette. Serve on plates with duck breast, cheese, and tomatoes arranged on top.

ALTERNATIVE CHEESES: Barinaga Txiki, River Falls Dante, Wisconsin Sheep Dairy Cooperative's Dante, Petit Basque, Abbaye de Bel'loc

WINE PAIRINGS: Pinot Noir, Beaujolais, Viognier, dry sherry

ADDITIONAL PAIRINGS FOR THE CHEESE: sour cherries, orange marmalade, hazelnuts, olives

EARLY AUTUMN PASTA SALAD
WITH FISCALINI BANDAGE WRAPPED CHEDDAR AND FUYU PERSIMMONS

SERVES 4

8 ounces farro-based pasta (use a small pasta such as rotini, elbows, or pizzichi)

2 large Fuyu persimmons, peeled, chopped into ½-inch cubes

1 large Granny Smith apple, peeled, cored, and chopped into ½-inch cubes

3 tablespoons honey

3 tablespoons lemon juice

Freshly ground black pepper

Sea salt

4 ounces Fiscalini Bandage Wrapped Cheddar

FUYU PERSIMMONS ARE ONE OF THE EARLY SIGNS THAT AUTUMN IS APPROACHING. They come into season, in shades of pale yellow to ocher to bright orange, just as the chill winds set in. They're exceptionally flavorful even when young; you'll find them musky and sweet, and they become only more so with age.

We find that Fiscalini Bandage Wrapped Cheddar is a mighty fine pairing for persimmons: salty and sweet, sharp and mellow, grassy and fruity. The wheaty taste of farro adds an element of autumn earthiness, while Granny Smith apples tart up the dish just a touch. We find that this recipe makes for a perfectly balanced meal—light yet satisfying—for when the air turns brisk.

1. Cook the pasta in a large pot of salted boiling water until al dente. Drain through a colander and rinse with cool water to stop the cooking process. Drain again and set aside. Toss it every so often to prevent sticking.

2. Toss the pasta, persimmons, apple cubes, honey, and lemon juice in a large bowl. Add freshly ground black pepper and sea salt to taste. Add more honey and lemon if you like.

3. Divide salad evenly among four plates. Using a cheese plane or vegetable peeler, cut long, thin swaths of the Fiscalini Bandage Wrapped Cheddar over each salad. Serve.

ALTERNATIVE CHEESES: Beecher's Flagship Reserve, Cabot Clothbound Cheddar, Keen's Cheddar, Montgomery's Cheddar, any stout aged Cheddar

WINE PAIRINGS: Viognier, Chardonnay, Syrah, Rhône Valley blends

ADDITIONAL PAIRINGS FOR THE CHEESE: chutney, mustard, green olives

SAVORY SHEEP'S-MILK RICOTTA
WITH RASPBERRIES AND CAPELLINI

SERVES 4

½ cup olive oil

¾ cup mashed raspberries

3 tablespoons lemon zest
Sea salt

16 ounces spaghetti or capellini

2 cups sheep's-milk ricotta

¼ teaspoon freshly ground
black pepper

½ teaspoon sugar

6 cups chopped dandelion
greens
Additional sea salt and
freshly ground black pepper

2 teaspoons lemon juice

ALTERNATIVE CHEESES:
Any rich, lush cow's-milk
ricotta will work in this
dish.

WINE PAIRINGS: Sauvi-
gnon Blanc, Tocai
Friulano, Orvieto,
Muscadet (Melon de
Bourgogne)

ADDITIONAL PAIRINGS
FOR THE CHEESE: roasted
almonds, blackberries,
basil, plums

SHEEP'S-MILK RICOTTA IS ONE OF THOSE LUSCIOUS DAIRY TREATS THAT STRADDLE THE savory-sweet line with aplomb. Fatty, rich, and full of signature sheep's-milk flavor, this ricotta is just as comfortable in a meaty lasagna as it is in a delicate fruit pastry.

To celebrate the diversity of this special cheese, we've created a savory dish with flavors normally reserved for dessert. Don't let the ingredient list fool you; despite the potential for confectionary leanings, this dish is absolutely worthy of being your go-to light outdoor dinner. Raspberries and lemon zest create a refreshing blend that will awaken your senses, while dandelion brings a touch of bitter balance to the table. Sheep's-milk ricotta creates a rich, creamy base for this delightfully textured dish, which cooks up in about 20 minutes. Can you say *quick and easy summer perfection?*

If you can't find dandelion greens, feel free to use arugula, escarole, or any other bitter greens you want. We like this dish with the raspberry seeds intact, but if you prefer, you can remove them from the fruit with a food mill before adding the berries to the sauce

1. Set a large pot of water to boil for the pasta. While waiting for the water to boil, heat olive oil in a saucepan on low heat for 3 minutes. Add raspberries and lemon zest. Continue to heat the oil and fruit for 5 minutes; the oil should not get so hot that it starts to sizzle and pop, but it should be hot enough that the flavor of the raspberries and lemon infuse the oil. If the oil gets too warm and the raspberries start to fry, remove from the heat for a minute to cool before continuing.

2. Once the pasta water boils, add salt and cook the pasta until just al dente. While the pasta is cooking, add the sheep's-milk ricotta, pepper, and sugar to the now-infused raspberry oil and continue cooking over low heat. Do not strain the raspberries out of the oil. Continue heating gently until the pasta is done cooking— the sauce should have a textured appearance and may look slightly broken. This is fine. When the pasta is cooked to al dente, drain through a colander and reserve ¼ cup of pasta water.

3. Add dandelion greens to the raspberry-ricotta sauce and cook just until the middle stems soften a bit. Stir the pasta and reserved pasta water into the sauce, 1 tablespoon at a time, until the sauce is a consistency you like; it should be relatively thick, but not clumpy. Season to taste with salt and pepper. Cook for 1 minute. Sprinkle with lemon juice, stir, and remove from heat. Serve immediately.

CHAPTER 3:
STOVETOP DELIGHTS

CHAPTER 3:
STOVETOP DELIGHTS

Smooth.

Creamy. Velvety. These are just a few ways to describe the sensuous texture of a freshly made stovetop macaroni-and-cheese dish. Whether your favorite mac memories were born from a blue box or your grandmother's carefully tended cream sauce, chances are you're familiar with the lush, buttery goodness that comes from simple preparation with a pot and a wooden spoon.

We are most definitely fans of traditional stovetop macaroni and cheese, and we've got more than a few tempting renditions that we're sharing in this chapter, but in the interest of creativity, we've spread our wings and explored the boundaries of traditional stovetop dishes.

Have you ever thought to mix blue cheese with salt-loving mussels? Fourme d'Ambert is a blue cheese that's more than up to the challenge. Or how about a hearty tomato soup that incorporates your favorite macaroni-and-cheese elements? We offer a version with Vella Dry Jack that approaches in a new way the velvety properties you're used to in a stovetop mac. Hungering for Mexican or Chinese food tonight? In this chapter, you'll find a few fried inter-national dishes that we're hoping will stretch your definition of macaroni and cheese. And of course, we've included many recipes to treat the creamy-mac-and-cheese purists among us.

One thing to remember when working on the stovetop: Do not walk away from your pot. Mornay sauce will clump in a matter of seconds, and anything dropped into hot oil is only a finger-snap away from burning. Stay focused on the project at hand—we guarantee you'll be repaid many times over with a meal well worth the five minutes of extra attention.

PETIT BASQUE WITH
ROASTED GARLIC, SHALLOTS, AND GEMELLI

- 2 whole heads garlic
- 4 tablespoons olive oil, divided
- ½ cup diced shallots (1 whole bulb)
- 8 ounces gemelli
- 1½ cups milk
- 2 tablespoons butter
- 2 tablespoons flour
- Sea salt
- Freshly ground black pepper
- 10 ounces Petit Basque, shredded
- 1 tablespoon chopped fresh chives

ALTERNATIVE CHEESES: Barinaga Ranch, Abbaye de Bel'loc, or a caramelly Basque-style cheese

WINE PAIRINGS: red Rhône blends, Cabernet Franc, Mencia

ADDITIONAL PAIRINGS FOR THE CHEESE: Serrano ham, polenta, roasted garlic, grapes

PETIT BASQUE IS A KICKER OF A CHEESE, SHEEPY TO THE CORE BUT STILL MAINTAINING a bit of French decorum. Paradoxically both outgoing and muted, Petit Basque lends a mild, nutty flavor with just a hint of fruit, and its somewhat Parmesan-like finish makes this cheese a contender when it comes to more intense cheese plates. In other words, Petit Basque is just as at home on a water cracker as it is over a bowl of chili con carne.

That said, this dish is an exercise in subtlety. Roasted garlic brings with it a touch of sweetness, while sautéed shallots provide a piquant allium note. Both flavors tame this spirited Basque beauty, resulting in a dish of delicate perfection.

1. Preheat oven to 400°F. Peel off most of the outer paper holding the garlic together. Trim off the top ¼ inch of the garlic with a sharp knife. Place the garlic in a small ramekin or other garlic-sized, ovenproof bowl and drizzle with 2 tablespoons of the olive oil. Cover ramekin loosely with foil and roast for 1 hour or until garlic is soft. Once the garlic is cool enough to handle, squeeze it out of its skin and mash it up with a fork.

2. In a small saucepan, heat the remaining 2 tablespoons of olive oil over medium-low heat. Add shallots and cook until they brown, about 4 minutes, stirring occasionally to keep them from burning. Remove from heat and set aside.

3. Cook the pasta in a large pot of salted boiling water until al dente. Drain through a colander and set aside.

4. To prepare the mornay sauce, heat the milk in a small saucepan over medium heat. As soon as the milk starts to steam and tiny bubbles form around the edges of the pan, turn off the heat. Place the butter in a medium saucepan and melt over medium flame. Add the flour and stir with a flat-edge wooden paddle just until the roux begins to take on a light brown color, scraping the bottom to prevent burning, about 3 minutes. Slowly add the milk and stir constantly until the sauce thickens enough to evenly coat the back of a spoon—a finger drawn along the back of the spoon should leave a clear swath. Add the mashed garlic cloves to the sauce, followed by the shallots and their cooking oil. Stir well.

5. Remove the sauce from heat and stir in salt and pepper. Add cheese to sauce, stirring until completely melted. Add pasta, folding until all noodles are covered with sauce. Stir in chives and season with salt and pepper to taste.

ROARING FORTIES WITH
HONEY-ROASTED DELICATA SQUASH, SAGE BUTTER, AND ROTINI

SERVES 4

¼   cup butter

3   tablespoons finely chopped fresh sage

¼   teaspoon sea salt

2   teaspoons honey

2   delicata squash, seeded and cut into small cubes (you do not need to peel)

10   ounces rotini

2   cups coarsely chopped pecans

10   ounces Roaring Forties blue cheese, rind removed, crumbled finely by hand

BLUE-CHEESE HATERS, STAND DOWN. ROARING FORTIES IS A FULL, PUNGENT, BRIGHT blue, but its honeyed flavor and delightful aftertaste make it a winner with even the most stubborn anti-mold folk. Originating Down Under, off the coast of Tasmania, this Australian blue cheese comes from around latitude 40 degrees south, an area known for its roaringly loud and powerful winds—hence the cheese's name.

Smooth and creamy, Roaring Forties is perfectly comfortable in either sweet or savory situations, so in this dish we opted to combine the two. Sweet delicata squash is roasted until caramelized with honey and sage butter, then tossed with rotini and toasted pecans. When serving this dish, make sure that you've distributed the cheese crumbles evenly, otherwise some diners will get a lot more blue than they've bargained for while others will be left wanting more.

1. Preheat oven to 375°F. In a small saucepan, melt butter over low heat. Add sage, salt, and honey. Cook, stirring constantly, for 3 minutes. Remove from heat and add squash, tossing to coat squash completely with butter. Pour squash and butter into an 8-by-8-inch baking dish, making sure to get as much butter out of the saucepan and into the baking dish as possible. Bake the squash until it is soft and caramelized, about 60 minutes, making sure to give the whole thing a good stir about halfway through for even roasting.

2. Cook the pasta in a large pot of salted boiling water until al dente. Drain through a colander and set aside.

3. While the pasta is cooking, add pecans to a small sauté pan. Heat over medium-low heat, tossing occasionally, until pecans become fragrant and just barely darken, about 4 minutes.

4. Add pasta and cheese to the baking dish with the squash, tossing well. Make sure there are no oversize chunks of blue cheese, unless your diners really like a mouthful of this lovely—and strong—stuff. Serve immediately in bowls, topped generously with toasted pecans.

ALTERNATIVE CHEESES: No Name Blue Cheese, Dolcelatte Blue Cheese

WINE PAIRINGS: Viognier, Chardonnay

ADDITIONAL PAIRINGS FOR THE CHEESE: roasted peaches, raspberries, honeycomb

SURFING GOAT CHÈVRE WITH
CHERRY TOMATOES, SPINACH, DILL, AND GEMELLI

SERVES 4

1	cup halved cherry tomatoes
12	ounces gemelli
2	cups whole milk
2	tablespoons butter
2	tablespoons flour
¼	teaspoon sea salt
¼	teaspoon freshly ground white pepper
2	cups chopped baby spinach
1	tablespoon finely chopped fresh dill, plus more for garnish
2	teaspoons lemon zest—about the zest of 1 lemon
8	ounces Surfing Goat Udderly Delicious chèvre, crumbled
4	ounces Monterey Jack, shredded
	Lemon juice for garnish

ALTERNATIVE CHEESES:
Any high-quality chèvre will do for this dish, as will any high-quality Monterey Jack. Ask your local cheesemonger for a recommendation.

WINE PAIRINGS:
Sauvignon Blanc, Grüner Veltliner, dry rosé

ADDITIONAL PAIRINGS FOR THE CHEESE:
slow-roasted tomatoes, eggplant, tarragon

OH, CHÈVRE, THAT CREAMY DELIGHT WE CHEESE LOVERS YEARN FOR. THERE'S JUST something about the luscious texture and slap-you-upside-the-head tang of a good goat cheese that calls to us through time and space, pulling our taste buds toward the light, like little Carol Anne Freeling in *Poltergeist*.

While we are lovers of almost any high-quality, small-production chèvre that crosses our palates, we've found that Hawaii's Surfing Goat Dairy produces a truly special variety. Called Udderly Delicious, this cheese is rich and goaty, grassy and pure; you can taste the pampered tropical joy of the goats that produce the milk for this dairy.

It's no secret that goat cheese pairs well with spinach, tomatoes, and lemon, but when melted into a creamy mornay sauce with a touch of Monterey Jack and poured over pasta, it takes your pleasure sensors to an all-time high. The crowning glory is humble dill, which wraps the dish up with a pretty green bow. Halle-luau!

1. Line a plate with four paper towels and set tomato halves cut side down on the plate. Set another plate on top of the tomatoes, and place a heavy weight on the plate to weigh it down—a cast-iron skillet or half-full kettle of water works great for this. Drain the tomatoes for 15 minutes, changing the paper towels once and pouring the liquid from the plate as necessary.

2. Cook the pasta in a large pot of salted boiling water until al dente. Drain through a colander, return pasta to pot, and set aside.

3. While the pasta is cooking, prepare the mornay sauce. Heat the milk in a small saucepan over medium heat. As soon as the milk starts to steam and tiny bubbles form around the edges of the pan, turn off the heat. Place the butter in a medium saucepan and melt over medium heat. Add the flour and stir with a flat-edge wooden paddle just until the roux begins to take on a light brown color, scraping the bottom to prevent burning, about 3 minutes. Slowly add the milk and stir constantly until the sauce thickens. Stir in salt, pepper, spinach, dill, and lemon zest, cooking for 2 minutes while stirring constantly. Remove from heat.

4. Add cheese to sauce, stirring constantly until completely melted. Pour sauce over pasta, tossing well to coat. Spoon into bowls and top generously with tomatoes, dusting each dish liberally with more dill. Sprinkle with additional lemon juice, if you like.

ROGUE RIVER BLUE WITH
CRAB SAUCE OVER FETTUCCINE

SERVES 6

- 16 ounces fettuccine
- 12 ounces cream cheese
- ¼ cup mayonnaise
- 1 teaspoon mustard powder
- 1 teaspoon smoked paprika
- ½ teaspoon cayenne pepper
- ½ teaspoon sea salt
- 2 cloves garlic, minced
- Zest of 1 medium lemon
- Juice of 1 medium lemon
- ¼ cup milk
- ⅓ cup dry white wine
- 2 tablespoons Worcestershire sauce
- 3 scallions, chopped
- 1 pound crabmeat, fresh or canned
- 8 ounces Rogue River Blue cheese, crumbled
- Hot sauce such as Sriracha or Tabasco for garnish
- Chopped fresh parsley for garnish

CRAB LOVES HOT SAUCE. HOT SAUCE LOVES BLUE CHEESE. THEREFORE, CRAB LOVES BLUE cheese. See? A completely logical reason to pair seafood and cheese.

Many of the blue cheeses produced by Rogue River Creamery in Oregon pair wonderfully with crab, which shouldn't be surprising since they both come into season during the colder months. Crumbled and tossed into a cheesy sauce, Rogue River gives prominence to the crab's sweetness, which in turn allows the piney-peppery tang of the blue to flourish.

This dish is wonderful served with whatever white wine you use for the sauce. Be sure to keep your favorite hot sauce nearby to punch it up a bit. If you don't have a double boiler, fill a 3-quart pot a third of the way with water and bring it to a boil. Place a metal bowl over it and—ta-da!—a makeshift double boiler.

1. Cook the pasta in a large pot of salted boiling water until al dente. Drain through a colander and set aside.

2. While the pasta cooks, start the sauce. Place the cream cheese, mayonnaise, mustard powder, paprika, cayenne, salt, and garlic in the top of a double boiler set over simmering water. Stir until the cream cheese is completely melted.

3. Slowly stir in the lemon zest, juice, milk, white wine, and Worcestershire sauce. Add the scallions and crabmeat and give the whole thing a good stir. Taste and adjust lemon juice, wine, and seasonings. Once the sauce is steaming, fold in the blue cheese and remove the top of the double boiler from the simmering water to stop the sauce from cooking—you want the blue cheese to swirl in and mix but not to melt completely.

4. Serve over plates of the fettuccine and garnish with hot sauce and chopped parsley.

ALTERNATIVE CHEESES: Oregonzola, Rogue River Reserve, Gorgonzola

WINE PAIRINGS: dry or semidry Chenin Blanc, or whatever wine you've used in the recipe

ADDITIONAL PAIRINGS FOR THE CHEESE: peas, roasted peaches

FETTUCCINE ALFREDO WITH
PARMESAN AND PECORINO

SERVES 4

16 ounces fettuccine

4 ounces (1 stick) butter, cut into quarters

2 cups heavy cream

¼ cup lemon juice, from 3 large lemons

3 ounces aged sheep's-milk Pecorino, finely grated

3 ounces Parmesan, finely grated

Pinch of sea salt

¼ teaspoon freshly ground black pepper

Pinch of fresh nutmeg

1 tablespoon lemon zest, from 1 medium lemon

2 cups fresh cherry tomatoes

Chopped fresh parsley to garnish

THERE'S NO WAY AROUND IT—FETTUCCINE ALFREDO IS NOT A DIET-FRIENDLY DISH. There are two cups of cream in here. Two cups of cheese. A whole stick of butter. Your personal trainer would beat you with a lead pipe if you ate this. But then again, his dinner probably consists of flaxseed-based protein shakes and an undressed salad. Sure, he may live a few years longer, but he did it without fettuccine Alfredo. Is that really living?

Using Pecorino along with the usual Parm is a refreshing change of pace; this aged sheep's-milk cheese will make the dish salty and luxuriously sheepy in flavor. As a follow-up, the acid from the lemon adds bright, sour notes to support all that creamy goodness.

1. Cook the pasta in a large pot of salted boiling water until al dente. Drain through a colander, reserving ¼ cup of the cooking water, and set aside.

2. Melt the butter in a large saucepan over medium heat. Once melted, add the cream and lemon juice. Cook for about 3 minutes, stirring occasionally. Add the cheeses, salt, pepper, nutmeg, and lemon zest, stirring until combined. Taste the sauce and adjust seasoning as needed. Add the pasta and tomatoes, tossing together until everything is well coated with sauce. If the sauce is too thick for you, add a bit of the reserved pasta water to thin it. Garnish with parsley.

ALTERNATIVE CHEESES: Everona Piedmont, Valley Shepherd's Ancient Shepherd

WINE PAIRINGS: Sangiovese, Chardonnay

ADDITIONAL PAIRINGS FOR THE CHEESE: chestnuts, honey, extra-virgin olive oil, Serrano ham

SQUID-INK PASTA WITH
MARINATED PERLINI MOZZARELLA

SERVES 4 TO 6

8 ounces perlini mozzarella

Zest of 2 medium lemons, divided

1 clove garlic, minced

Pinch of chili flakes

2 teaspoons chopped parsley

Olive oil

16 ounces squid-ink spaghetti or capellini

½ cup basil leaves, cut into chiffonade

Juice of 1 medium lemon

Maldon, fleur de sel, or other high-quality salt (do not use kosher or iodized salt)

YOU KNOW HOW MUCH WE LOVE CHEESE, BUT SOMETIMES WE NEED TO TAKE A MOMENT to focus on the pasta component in a mac-and-cheese dish. The first thing to notice about squid-ink pasta is its polished-obsidian color, which stupefies and intrigues most first-time eaters. Taste-wise, squid ink possesses a briny subtlety that infuses itself into the noodles. The flavor, because it is so delicate, is best treated simply—a bit of olive oil, a few wisps of lemon zest, a tangle of basil, and some briefly marinated perlini mozzarella.

This dish leaves room for creativity, so feel free to alter the marinade if you wish. Swap out the lemon for orange, or perhaps add a sprig of thyme. Regardless, keep it simple. Be sure to use high-moisture perlini mozzarella, the kind packed in water, as low-moisture mozzarella will be too firm for this dish.

1. Drain the water from the mozzarella and lightly pat dry with paper towels. Place in a bowl and add the zest of 1 lemon, garlic, chili flakes, and parsley. Drizzle lightly with olive oil until the mozzarella is well coated and stir ingredients together. Cover and marinate on the counter for 4 hours.

2. Cook the pasta in a large pot of salted boiling water until al dente. Drain through a colander.

3. Toss pasta with basil and serve on plates or in deep bowls. Make a depression in each mound of pasta and fill it with a few generous spoonfuls of the marinated mozzarella. Garnish plates with a drizzle of the cheese's marinade, the zest and juice of the other lemon, and fine sea salt. Serve immediately.

ALTERNATIVE CHEESES: Feel free to use larger mozzarella balls, but be sure to cut them into thin slices or wedges before marinating.

WINE PAIRINGS: Grechetto, Vermentino, Orvieto, Prosecco (sparkling)

ADDITIONAL PAIRINGS FOR THE CHEESE: herbed focaccia, heirloom tomatoes, toasted almonds, arugula

GRAND EWE WITH GOLDEN RAISINS,
PINE NUTS, AND MACARONI

SERVES 4

- 10 ounces elbow macaroni
- 1½ cups milk
- 2 tablespoons butter
- 2 tablespoons flour
- ¼ teaspoon sea salt
- ¼ teaspoon freshly ground black pepper
- 1 cup golden raisins
- 8 ounces Grand Ewe sheep's-milk Gouda, rind removed, shredded
- ¼ cup mascarpone
- 1 cup coarsely chopped pine nuts, toasted lightly, divided

SOME CHEESES ARE BEST LEFT AS IS, BUT GOUDA IS NOT NECESSARILY ONE OF THEM. Traditionally a cow's-milk cheese from the Netherlands, it has a solid milky flavor with just a touch of grit and butterscotch. How can you improve upon a classic as fine as this?

Well, the Dutch decided to push the envelope by creating a Gouda made entirely from sheep's milk. Aged for just one year, this version has a smooth texture with a hint of almond nuttiness. Vintage Grand Ewe, an exemplary sheep's-milk Gouda, takes on a richer, more elegant texture while still maintaining those signature caramel notes. Pairing the cheese with sweet golden raisins and the robust crunch of pine nuts produces a dish that is a dreamy, creamy fusion of flavor and texture.

1. Cook the pasta in a large pot of salted boiling water until al dente. Drain through a colander and set aside.

2. To prepare the mornay sauce, heat the milk in a small saucepan over medium heat. As soon as the milk starts to steam and tiny bubbles form around the edges of the pan, turn off the heat. Place the butter in a medium saucepan and melt over medium flame. Add the flour and stir with a flat-edge wooden paddle just until the roux begins to take on a light brown color, scraping the bottom to prevent burning, about 3 minutes. Slowly add the milk and stir constantly until the sauce thickens enough to evenly coat the back of a spoon—a finger drawn along the back of the spoon should leave a clear swath. Stir in salt, pepper, and golden raisins. Cook for 1 minute, stirring constantly. Remove from heat, add Gouda and mascarpone, and stir until completely melted. Season with more salt and pepper to taste.

3. Pour sauce over pasta and stir in half of the pine nuts. Serve in bowls, topped with the remaining pine nuts for garnish.

ALTERNATIVE CHEESES: Ewephoria sheep's-milk Gouda, Cypress Grove Lamb Chopper, or Trader Joe's generic sheep's-milk Gouda. If all else fails, you can use a regular cow's-milk Gouda, which will still shine.

WINE PAIRINGS: dry Riesling, Merlot

ADDITIONAL PAIRINGS FOR THE CHEESE: olives, prosciutto, apples

BRIGANTE WITH TILAPIA, SHALLOTS,
SPRING HERBS, AND FUSILLI

SERVES 2 TO 4

- **4** tablespoons butter, divided
- **¼** cup minced shallots
- **1** tablespoon chopped fresh tarragon
- **4** teaspoons chopped chervil
- **½** teaspoon coarsely ground black peppercorns
- **¼** cup dry white wine, such as Sauvignon Blanc
- **2** small tilapia fillets, about ½ pound total
- **8** ounces fusilli
- **2** cups milk
- **2** tablespoons flour
- **½** teaspoon sea salt
- **¼** teaspoon freshly ground black pepper
- **7** ounces Brigante, rind removed, grated

  Lemon wedges to garnish

ALTERNATIVE CHEESES: San Andreas, Berkswell, Shepherd's Way Friesago, Young Mahón

WINE PAIRINGS: Muscadet from the Loire Valley (Melon de Bourgogne grape), French Chardonnay, Sauvignon Blanc, Grechetto or Vermentino from Italy

ADDITIONAL PAIRINGS FOR THE CHEESE: Lucques or picholine olives, roasted red peppers with olive oil, smoked paprika

IN OUR OPINION, BRIGANTE IS THE KING OF PECORINOS. NUTTY AND SMOOTH WITH a sweet, buttery *aaaaaah* enveloping every bite, this Italian cheese very closely mimics the creamy goodness of cow's-milk cheeses. Recalcitrant cheese overlords might balk at calling it a Pecorino at all—with its amiable nature and creamy texture, it is unlike the generally dry, gritty cheeses often found in this family— but it is indeed made from the milk of Sardinian ewes, so the Pecorino title remains.

Wendy, my rock-star cheesemonger at the Oakland Whole Foods Market, knows a secret that no cheese lover or seafood fanatic could ever have guessed: tilapia and Brigante make for a stupendous macaroni and cheese. Brigante's creamy tang supports the tender texture of the delicate white fish without drowning its sea-life sweetness. Shallots bring a little allium *saveur* to the table, while tarragon and chervil lend a perfect green springtime twist to this fresh, creamy dish. Feel free to substitute shrimp for tilapia if you like.   —SS

1. In a sauté pan, melt 1 tablespoon of butter over medium heat. Add shallots and cook until soft, then add tarragon, chervil, and pepper. Cook for 1 minute, stirring constantly, then add white wine. Cook, still stirring constantly, until a good amount of the liquid has cooked off—about 2 minutes. Transfer shallots and herbs to a small bowl and return the pan to the stove.

2. In the same sauté pan—do not rinse it—add 1 tablespoon of butter and turn heat to medium. Sauté tilapia fillets for 3 minutes on each side, making sure to get a nice, crispy layer where the fish touches the pan. Transfer to a bowl and shred coarsely with two forks. Set aside.

3. Cook the pasta in a large pot of salted boiling water until al dente. Drain through a colander and set aside.

4. To prepare the mornay sauce, heat the milk in a small saucepan over medium heat. As soon as the milk starts to steam and tiny bubbles form around the edges of the pan, turn off the heat. Place the remaining 2 tablespoons of butter in a medium saucepan and melt over medium flame. Add the flour and stir with a flat-edge wooden paddle just until the roux begins to take on a light brown color, scraping the bottom to prevent burning, about 3 minutes. Slowly add the milk and stir constantly until the sauce thickens enough to evenly coat the back of a spoon—a finger drawn along the back of the spoon should leave a clear swath. Lower heat to medium-low, add salt, pepper, and sautéed shallots and herbs. Remove from heat and add cheese to sauce, stirring until completely melted.

5. In a large bowl, add pasta to the mornay and toss to coat. Gently fold in the shredded fish; you don't want to smash it. Serve hot and garnish with lemon wedges.

MUSSELS IN WHITE WINE BROTH
WITH FOURME D'AMBERT AND ROTINI

SERVES 4

2 pounds Prince Edward Island mussels

8 ounces rotini

2 tablespoons butter

1 onion, chopped

2 cloves garlic, minced

1½ cups dry white wine, such as Sauvignon Blanc

¼ teaspoon freshly ground black pepper

6 ounces Fourme d'Ambert, crumbled

Juice of 1 lemon

¼ cup parsley, chopped

Dash of finishing salt such as Maldon or sel gris (do not use iodized table salt)

A loaf of crusty bread for serving

ALTERNATIVE CHEESES: Gorgonzola Dolce, Cashel Blue, Roquefort, Cambozola

WINE PAIRINGS: dry Chenin Blanc, sparkling Chenin Blanc, dry rosé

ADDITIONAL PAIRINGS FOR THE CHEESE: *membrillo* (quince jam), apple butter

THERE'S A SUPPOSEDLY IRREFUTABLE LAW IN THE FOOD WORLD THAT YOU SHOULDN'T—can't, in fact—combine cheese with seafood. Who knows who came up with this rule and why, but if you're one of the officers who uphold this antiquated prohibition, well, you haven't tasted mussels in blue-cheese broth.

Mussels, an affordable, sustainable, and tasty food if there ever was one, give up their saline liquor when steamed in a combination of white wine and Fourme d'Ambert. An ancient French cheese, Fourme d'Ambert possesses hints of earth, a touch of black pepper, and a luxurious creaminess that complements the ocean flavor of the mussels well. The broth is intensely addicting, and you will want some crusty bread to mop up every last drop.

1. Soak the mussels in a large pot of cold water for about 30 minutes to coax them into spitting out any sand or grit they may be hiding. Toss out the water and cover the mussels again with fresh cold water for another 10 minutes to encourage them to cleanse themselves a bit more.

2. Debeard the mussels by taking their byssal threads (their "beards") and giving them a good yank until they come off. Discard the beards and set the mussels aside. Toss any mussels that aren't closed, as these are already dead and not edible.

3. Cook the pasta in a large pot of salted boiling water until al dente. Drain through a colander and set aside.

4. While the pasta cooks, place a large pot over medium-high heat. Add the butter and allow to melt. Once the butter begins to bubble a bit, add the onion and garlic. Cook over medium-high heat, stirring occasionally, until the onions have softened a bit.

5. Add the white wine and pepper. Bring to a boil and add the Fourme d'Ambert. Once the cheese melts into the wine, lower the heat to medium and add the mussels. Cover the pot with a tight-fitting lid and cook for about 6 or 7 minutes, being sure to give the mussels a stir after about 4 minutes. Discard any mussels that are closed, as these were dead before cooking. Some may be only slightly open; if you have to debate about whether it's good to eat or not, toss it— better safe than sorry. Remove from heat.

6. Squeeze lemon juice over the mussels and toss together with the parsley and finishing salt. Spoon the pasta into wide bowls, generously ladling mussels and broth over it. Serve immediately with hunks of the crusty bread and go to town.

BEECHER'S FLAGSHIP CHEDDAR
WITH AVOCADO, LIME, AND SHELL PASTA

SERVES 4 TO 6

- 1 jalapeño pepper
- Zest of 1 lime
- Juice of 1 lime
- 2 green onions, green parts only, chopped
- 2 cloves garlic, chopped
- 3 ripe avocados, pits and skin removed, divided
- 10 ounces conchiglie or other medium shell pasta
- 1½ cups milk
- 2 tablespoons butter
- 3 tablespoons flour
- 1 teaspoon sea salt
- ½ teaspoon freshly ground black pepper
- 10 ounces Beecher's Flagship Cheddar, shredded
- ¼ cup chopped cilantro
- Lime wedges for garnish

IF YOU EVER HAVE THE OPPORTUNITY TO WANDER THROUGH THE PIKE PLACE MARKET, the heart of the food scene in Seattle, you'll likely come across the Beecher's Handmade Cheese shop. Inside, you can sample their wares and watch the cheesemaking process unfold before your eyes. The proprietors serve what they call the World's Best mac and cheese; with its jaunty kick of spice and smooth sauce, it's definitely a contender for the title.

We love to use Beecher's Flagship—a fierce, creamy paragon of Cheddar if ever there was one—in this avocado macaroni and cheese. The svelte texture of avocado melds so well with this sharp, tangy Cheddar. Smooth and buttery with a slight citrus tang, this jade-colored mac is a casual way to enjoy mac and cheese.

1. Remove the stem from the jalapeño and cut the jalapeño in half. Remove the ribs and seeds—or keep them, depending on how much heat you like. Toss the jalapeño into the bowl of a food processor with the lime zest and lime juice. Add green onions, garlic, and flesh of 2 of the avocados. Blitz together into a very smooth paste.

2. Cook the pasta in a large pot of salted boiling water until al dente. Drain through a colander and set aside.

3. To prepare the mornay sauce, heat the milk in a small saucepan over medium heat. As soon as the milk starts to steam and tiny bubbles form around the edges of the pan, turn off the heat. Place the butter in a medium saucepan and melt over medium flame. Add the flour and stir with a flat-edge wooden paddle just until the roux begins to take on a light brown color, scraping the bottom to prevent burning, about 3 minutes. Slowly add the milk and stir constantly until the sauce thickens enough to evenly coat the back of a spoon—a finger drawn along the back of the spoon should leave a clear swath. Remove from heat and stir in salt and pepper. Add cheese to sauce, stirring until completely melted. Add the avocado-onion paste and whisk together until uniform and creamy. The key word here, if you haven't guessed, is smooth. Season with more salt and pepper to taste.

4. Add the pasta and cilantro to the sauce and stir together. Dice the last avocado and toss together with the mac and cheese. Serve immediately with a splash of lime juice.

ALTERNATIVE CHEESES: Jasper Hill Cabot Clothbound Cheddar, Fiscalini Bandage Wrapped Cheddar, Shelburne Reserve

WINE PAIRINGS: Pinot Grigio, Verdelho, Godello

ADDITIONAL PAIRINGS FOR THE CHEESE: corn, cooked black beans, persimmons, most chili peppers, winter squashes such as pumpkin or butternut

TOMATO SOUP WITH STAR PASTA
AND VELLA DRY JACK CRISPS

SERVES 4 TO 6

1   (28-ounce) can whole plum tomatoes

¼   cup olive oil, divided

Sea salt

Freshly ground black pepper

1   white onion, diced

2   cloves garlic, minced

1½   cups vegetable broth

1   teaspoon sugar

1   whole sprig of thyme

¼   cup coarsely chopped basil leaves

3   ounces stelline or other small star-shaped pasta

5   ounces Vella Dry Jack, finely grated, divided

TOMATO SOUP FROM A CAN IS LAME. THERE, WE SAID IT. TO HECK WITH NOSTALGIA. It's almost always too salty; the tomatoes have lost any bounce in flavor they once had; the taste is flat; and, and . . . need we go on? The homemade stuff is where it's at. Roasted tomatoes are smoky, fruity, and perky. This soup is comfort food at its finest, and it's easy to make.

Our tomato soup is filled with adorable star pasta and dotted with Vella Dry Jack cheese, served two ways—raw and baked. Vella Dry Jack is a Monterey Jack cheese made by the Vella Cheese Company in Sonoma, California. The cheese is aged for an exceptionally long time and rubbed with a combination of safflower oil, unsweetened cocoa, and black pepper. The rub doesn't flavor the cheese, but it does give the rind the striking appearance of varnished wood.

The flavor of Vella Dry Jack is caramelly and balanced when raw, but when the cheese is baked into snappy crisps, its flavor transforms into something jazzy and exuberantly salty. A pleasant contrast in textures makes this a welcome departure from grocery-store canned tomato soup. Go ahead, prove us wrong.

1. Set a rack to the middle of the oven and preheat to 450°F. Drain the tomatoes over a bowl and reserve all the juices they give up plus anything extra from the can. Place the tomatoes on a baking sheet lined with parchment paper, drizzle with 2 tablespoons of the olive oil, and season with salt and black pepper. Roast for 20 to 25 minutes (you want the tomatoes to char a bit). When finished, remove from the oven and drop the oven temperature to 350°F.

2. Pour the remaining olive oil into a large pot and set over medium-high heat. Sauté the onions and garlic until soft and fragrant. Add the tomatoes and their reserved juices, vegetable broth, sugar, and thyme. Bring to a boil and reduce heat to low. Simmer uncovered for 30 minutes, stirring occasionally.

3. Remove the thyme and add the basil. Working in batches, process the soup in a blender until smooth. Be careful—hot steam can blow the lid off the blender and send napalm-like liquid everywhere. (If you have an immersion blender, you can process the soup right in the pot.) Pour the soup back into the pot, bring back to a boil, add pasta, and simmer for 7 minutes or until pasta is al dente.

4. While the soup cooks, makes Vella crisps. Take 3 ounces of the cheese and place heaping tablespoons a few inches apart on a baking sheet lined with parchment paper or a silicone mat. Bake for 13 to 15 minutes, until golden and crisp. Allow to cool. You should get about 15 crisps. » recipe continues

5. Serve soup in bowls with the crisps and the remaining grated cheese. The crisps are lovely as an accompaniment, whether eaten straight, used for dipping, or crumbled into the soup.

ALTERNATIVE CHEESES: Spring Hill Dry Jack, Parmesan

WINE PAIRINGS: Gamay, Barbera

ADDITIONAL PAIRINGS FOR THE CHEESE: buckwheat, rosemary, sun-dried tomatoes

"AND CALLED IT MACARONI"

Yankee Doodle went to town,
Riding on a pony;
Stuck a feather in his hat,
And called it Macaroni.

WHO IS YANKEE DOODLE, ANYWAY? AND what does frilly headgear have to do with melty bowls of macaroni and cheese? Surely every American child has sung the song "Yankee Doodle" and wondered what it meant.

Yankee was used by the British (and others, especially the Dutch) as a pejorative term for an American. During the Revolutionary War, it was a particularly popular way for the British to describe the ragtag colonists. *Doodle* is another word for "fool."

As for macaroni? Well, *macaroni* was the slang term for a British dandy or fop. (Picture men in three-foot-high fancy wigs, lots of powder on their faces, epicene mannerisms, and mincing gaits.) The word *macaroni* was also used by such characters to describe the eighteenth-century equivalent of haute couture.

So, "Yankee Doodle" is essentially about a clueless American putting a feather in his dingy old hat and thinking it incredibly cool and stylish. Early Yankees eventually adopted the song and added their own star-spangled lyrics in the hopes of lifting spirits and rallying patriotic pride.

The song, as you see, has nothing to do with pasta and cheese.

SOBA NOODLES WITH PARMESAN
AND PAN-SEARED BRUSSELS SPROUTS

SERVES 2 AS AN ENTRÉE,
4 AS A SIDE

8 ounces soba noodles

2 tablespoons grapeseed oil,
divided (olive oil will work
just fine too)

About 20 small Brussels
sprouts, stems and loose
outer leaves discarded

Fine-grained sea salt

Coarsely ground black
pepper

Pinch of chili flakes

2 cloves garlic, minced

4 ounces Parmesan,
finely grated

FOR YEARS, I ATTENDED GRADUATE SCHOOL FULL-TIME AT NIGHT AND WORKED A full-time job in a nonprofit adoption service during the day. Any extra time I had between the two was spent doing homework, trying to keep a blog moderately up-to-date, attempting to pound out freelance food-writing assignments, keeping the fire in my relationship burning, and reviving my otherwise nearly comatose social life. Cooking, sadly, becomes an afterthought when you have a paper due and you're assuring your best friend that, no, you haven't fallen off the face of the earth.

This recipe was a happy accident that I stumbled upon when I was trying to throw something together for dinner; in a haze, I just grabbed at whatever was closest to me. It was so simple and satisfying that it quickly became part of my regular dinner rotation in autumn, when Brussels sprouts are in season. —GM

1. Prepare the soba noodles per the manufacturer's instructions. Once they are cooked, immediately drain and rinse under cool water for a moment, drain again, and then toss with 1 tablespoon of grapeseed oil. Do this regardless of what the soba noodle instructions say at that point, as some may instruct you not to add oil. Set aside.

2. Place the remaining tablespoon of grapeseed oil in a skillet over medium-high heat. When the oil is hot and shimmering, add the Brussels sprouts. Season with salt, pepper, and chili flakes. Cook, stirring occasionally, until the surfaces of the sprouts start to turn golden brown and they soften a bit, about 7 to 10 minutes. Add the garlic and cook until fragrant, about 30 seconds.

3. Toss the soba noodles in the hot pan for about 30 seconds. Remove from heat and add an extra glug of oil, if you desire. Plate and cover with a robust amount of Parmesan. Serve immediately.

ALTERNATIVE CHEESES: Vella Dry Jack, Grana Padano

WINE PAIRINGS: Grüner Veltliner, Tocai Friulano

ADDITIONAL PAIRINGS FOR THE CHEESE: freshly ground black pepper, red pepper flakes, fava beans

PENNE WITH ETORKI CREAM SAUCE
AND ASPARAGUS

SERVES 2 AS AN ENTRÉE,
4 AS A SIDE

10 ounces penne rigate

1 cup half-and-half

1 tablespoon butter

1½ tablespoons flour

¼ teaspoon sea salt

Freshly ground black pepper

½ pound Etorki, rind removed,
cut into ½-inch cubes

1 tablespoon olive oil

1 pound fresh asparagus,
trimmed and the bottom
halves of stalks peeled

ETORKI IS A LOVELY BASQUE CHEESE THAT ORIGINATES IN THE FRENCH PYRÉNÉES-
Atlantiques area. Made from sheep's milk, this rich, nutty cheese shares some
sweet tones with Gouda, but its creamy bite makes it unique in its class. Right
away, you'll note Etorki's signature burned-caramel flavor, which is part of what
makes this cheese so special. Treat it as you would a perfect, caramel-kissed
Scotch, one that deserves to be savored in tiny tastes.

In creating this recipe, we leaned toward simplicity: the pasta is paired only
with sautéed asparagus. We use half-and-half in the mornay sauce instead of
milk, which gives this dish an ethereal texture, so smooth and velvety that it
seems to lift off the plate and into the clouds.

1. Cook the pasta in a large pot of salted boiling water until al dente. Drain through
a colander and set aside.

2. To prepare the mornay sauce, heat the half-and-half in a small saucepan over
medium heat. As soon as the half-and-half starts to steam and tiny bubbles form
around the edges of the pan, turn off the heat. Place the butter in a medium saucepan
and melt over medium flame. Add the flour and stir with a flat-edge wooden paddle
just until the roux begins to take on a light brown color, scraping the bottom to
prevent burning, about 3 minutes. Slowly add the half-and-half and stir constantly
until the sauce thickens enough to evenly coat the back of a spoon—a finger drawn
along the back of the spoon should leave a clear swath. Remove from heat and stir in
salt and pepper. Add cheese to sauce, stirring until completely melted.

3. In a heavy frying pan, heat olive oil over medium heat. Sauté asparagus until the
stalks are bright green and take on a nice browned color in places. They should be
tender enough to bite but not soggy. Remove from heat.

4. Serve by placing a few large spoonfuls of pasta on a plate and laying the asparagus
across the top. If the cheese sauce has cooled, heat it gently over low heat until it is a
pourable consistency. Pour a generous amount of the cheese sauce over the asparagus,
letting it run down into the pasta.

ALTERNATIVE CHEESES: Black-Eyed Susan, Petit Basque, Abbaye de Bel'loc,
Abbaye de Tamié, Ossau-Iraty

WINE PAIRINGS: Grüner Veltliner, Tocai Friulano

ADDITIONAL PAIRINGS FOR THE CHEESE: heirloom tomatoes, potatoes, artichokes

CHILI-MAC WITH REDWOOD HILL
SMOKED GOAT CHEDDAR

SERVES 4 TO 6

For the spice paste:

2 tablespoons red chili powder

1½ teaspoons ground chipotle chili powder

1½ teaspoons ancho chili powder

1 teaspoon smoked paprika

1½ tablespoons ground cumin

2 teaspoons ground coriander

2 heaping teaspoons chopped fresh oregano

2 teaspoons chopped fresh thyme

¼ teaspoon freshly ground black pepper

5 tablespoons water

For the chili:

6 strips raw thick-cut bacon, chopped

2 pounds chuck roast, cut into ½-inch cubes

Sea salt

1 red onion, chopped

4 cloves garlic, minced

2 jalapeño peppers, seeds and ribs discarded, minced

1 cup chopped cilantro leaves

1 (14-ounce) can diced tomatoes

2 teaspoons brown sugar

4 cups water

Juice of 1 lime, divided

10 ounces spiral pasta

1 tablespoon cornstarch, mixed with 3 tablespoons cold water

12 ounces Redwood Hill Smoked Goat Cheddar, shredded

TWO PEOPLE TAUGHT US THE CRUCIAL FACTORS THAT MAKE HEARTY CHILI. HANK SHAW, a hunter and forager of inspiring abilities, taught us the importance of a balanced and well-contemplated spice blend; and Harry Palmer, a chili-competition junkie living in Sacramento, imparted to us the sagacity of smoke, which can truly gild the chili pot.

Unfortunately, not everyone is able to smoke his or her own meat, and the flavor of liquid smoke becomes acrid when used with a heavy hand. A high-quality smoked cheese can remedy this con carne conundrum.

Redwood Hill Farm, a goat dairy in Sonoma, California, is known for a number of very respectable cheeses, but its smoked goat Cheddar is truly astounding. Creamy with a pleasant bite, the cheese has a robust smokiness that doesn't disappear in a bowl of chili. This is one of the best smoked Cheddars out there, hands down.

1. Make the spice paste by mixing the chili powder, chipotle powder, ancho powder, smoked paprika, cumin, coriander, oregano, thyme, pepper, and water in a bowl and giving it all a quick stir. Set aside.

2. Cook the bacon in a 4- to 6-quart thick-bottomed pot until quite crispy. (The bacon will soften a bit later, during cooking.) Drain on a plate lined with paper towels and set aside. Reserve all of the bacon grease from the pan in a bowl or jar.

3. Place 2 tablespoons of the bacon grease back into the pot. Over medium-high heat and working in batches, sear the beef until nicely browned on all sides, salting every so often. Be sure not to crowd the beef; if you do, it won't sear, it will steam, which you don't want.

4. When all the meat is seared, lower the heat to medium, add another tablespoon of bacon grease (perhaps do so while jogging in place to burn off a few calories?), and add the onions. Stir only a few times so the onions soften but develop some color to them. After about 6 minutes, add the garlic and jalapeños, then cook, stirring, until fragrant, about 30 seconds.

5. Add the spice paste and cook for about 30 seconds. Some of the paste will stick to the bottom of the pan; don't fret about it, as it will come off shortly.

6. Add the cilantro, tomatoes, brown sugar, water, and half the lime juice. Bring to a boil over high heat, reduce the heat to medium-low, and simmer, covered, for 90 minutes.

7. Add the pasta. Cover and cook for 6 to 10 more minutes, until the pasta is al dente. Taste the chili and adjust spices or sugar if necessary. Add the cornstarch slurry and the rest of the lime juice, stirring until thick. If your chili has cooked down significantly, feel free to omit the cornstarch. Serve with generous amounts of cheese.

ALTERNATIVE CHEESES: Tillamook Smoked Cheddar, Carr Valley Apple Smoked Cheddar, Winters Cheese Co. Smoked Cheddar, Emerald Valley Artisans Smoked Cheddar (many smoked Cheddars work here, but in our opinion, the smokier the better)

WINE PAIRINGS: Rhône Valley blends, Syrah, Zinfandel

ADDITIONAL PAIRINGS FOR THE CHEESE: toasted almonds, fresh Mexican chorizo, smoked paprika (caliente or dulce)

A MODERN DAIRY: REDWOOD HILL FARM

WHEN MOST AMERICANS THINK OF A modern dairy, all sorts of unsavory images come to mind. Huge concrete-gray facilities, robotlike milking devices made of metal tubes and tanks, animals crammed ear to ear with no access to grazing land. Modern dairy farming has gotten a bad rep, and for good reason: We've all seen images of large-scale commercial dairy operations and the abysmal living conditions the creatures raised on some of these farms endure.

Thankfully, there's a new generation of dairy farmers who adhere to a different ethic. Located in Sebastopol, California, Redwood Hill Farm takes advantage of all the conveniences of modern technology while maintaining a pastoral setting for its livestock.

Jennifer and Scott Bice, the sister-and-brother team that runs Redwood Hill Farm, are committed to three things above all else: the health of their animals, the quality of their product, and minimizing their impact on the environment. To boost the farm's sustainability points, 100 percent of the energy consumed by the Redwood Hill dairy operation is offset by nearly two acres of rooftop solar panels.

In addition to all this, Redwood Hill is the first goat dairy in the country to be Certified Humane by the Humane Farm Animal Care organization for the treatment of its livestock. This just goes to show that modern technology and ethically responsible farming practices do not need to be mutually exclusive—they may even go hand in hand, like chèvre and honey.

TOMA MACARONI EGG ROLLS
WITH SPICY-SWEET DIPPING SAUCE

MAKES 24 EGG ROLLS

4   ounces elbow macaroni

½   cup whole milk

2   teaspoons fish sauce

1   tablespoon butter

1   tablespoon flour

4   ounces Point Reyes Toma, shredded

24 (4-by-4-inch) egg-roll wrappers

    Sriracha hot sauce

2   green onions, halved lengthwise and cut into thin 1-inch-long matchsticks

    Vegetable, canola, or grapeseed oil for frying

POINT REYES TOMA IS ONE OF THOSE TABLE CHEESES THAT ARE PRACTICALLY PERFECT in every way. It's easy to eat, pleases everyone's palate, and pairs well with pretty much anything. Here, Toma is melted into a simple mornay made extra savory with an ingredient no one will guess: fish sauce, which adds a pleasing umami tang. The macaroni is tucked tightly into egg-roll wrappers with a few wisps of green onion and a hint of Sriracha. This is a groovy way to serve mac and cheese at a party, and the sweet-sour-spicy dipping sauce takes it over the top.

Be sure to plan ahead, as the macaroni needs to chill at least several hours before it can be cut and rolled up in the egg-roll wrappers. To ensure crispy egg rolls, keep the folds tight, with few flaps or pockets where oil can sneak in and make the roll soggy.

1. Cook the pasta until al dente in a pot of salted boiling water. Drain and set aside.

2. To prepare the mornay sauce, heat the milk and fish sauce in a small saucepan over medium heat. As soon as it starts to steam and tiny bubbles form around the edges of the pan, turn off the heat. Place the butter in a medium saucepan and melt over medium flame. Add the flour and stir with a flat-edge wooden paddle just until the roux begins to take on a light brown color, scraping the bottom to prevent burning, about 3 minutes. Slowly add the milk and stir constantly until the sauce thickens enough to evenly coat the back of a spoon—a finger drawn along the back of the spoon should leave a clear swath. Remove from heat and add cheese to sauce, stirring until completely melted.

3. Stir the pasta into the sauce and place in an 8-by-8-inch baking dish. Cool to room temperature before covering with plastic wrap, then chill in the fridge for at least 4 hours to overnight.

4. Cut the chilled macaroni in the pan into small rectangles by making 4 even cuts vertically and 6 cuts horizontally. Place a bit of water in a bowl and set aside.

5. To roll the egg rolls, lay a wrapper in front of you with a corner pointing upward so you have a diamond shape. Squeeze a small dot of the Sriracha on the wrapper near the point closest to you. Place a few pieces of green onion and a piece of cut macaroni and cheese just a bit below the middle of the wrapper so that the longer side is parallel to you. Lift the bottom corner up over the macaroni rectangle and begin tightly rolling until you reach the center. Tightly fold in the left and right corners toward the center, then continue rolling up. Dip your fingers in a bit of water and moisten the top corner, then finish rolling. The wet tip will glue itself to the roll. Set aside and finish the remaining egg rolls. ❱❱ recipe continues

6. To fry, fill a wok or heavy-bottomed pan with 2 inches of oil. Heat oil over medium heat until it reaches 350°F. Use a candy/fryer thermometer for this; if you don't have one, a nifty trick is to throw a 1-inch cube of bread into the oil. When it turns golden brown in 60 seconds, the oil is ready. When the oil is at temperature, fry the egg rolls 4 or 5 at a time, about 90 seconds for each batch or until brown and crispy. Remove from oil using a slotted spoon and cool on a wire rack. It's best to place paper towels under the rack to make cleanup easier.

SPICY-SWEET DIPPING SAUCE

MAKES ⅔ CUP

- ¼ **cup sweet chili sauce**
- ¼ **cup white vinegar**
- 1 **tablespoon brown sugar**
- 2 **teaspoons soy sauce**
- 1 **tablespoon ketchup**
- 2 **teaspoons cornstarch mixed into 1 tablespoon cold water**

1. Heat the chili sauce, white vinegar, brown sugar, soy sauce, and ketchup in a saucepan over medium-high heat until well mixed. Remove from heat and add the cornstarch slurry and whisk together. Place in a bowl and serve with egg rolls.

ALTERNATIVE CHEESES: Taleggio, Raclette, Morbier, Fontina

WINE PAIRINGS: sparkling Chenin Blanc from Vouvray, Crémant de Loire or Crémant d'Alsace rosé, Riesling (dry or sweet)

ADDITIONAL PAIRINGS FOR THE CHEESE: flatbread, pizza, tapenade, persimmons, honeydew

KÄSESPÄTZLE

SERVES 4

2 tablespoons butter

½ medium onion, sliced

A few tablespoons water

3 large eggs, beaten

¼ cup plus 3 tablespoons heavy cream, divided

1½ cups flour

½ teaspoon sea salt

¼ teaspoon freshly ground black pepper

8 ounces Edam, shredded

PRONOUNCED "KAY-ZEH-SHPET-ZLEH," THIS DISH IS A GREAT EXAMPLE OF TRADITIONAL German comfort food. It consists of only tiny dumpling-like noodles and melty, stretchy cheese that wants nothing more than to cling to your face and hands. Really, can a dish get any homier?

This recipe calls for Edam, a lovely Dutch cheese from northern Holland. Young Edam is soft and mild but gets harder and sharper as it ages. We prefer a young cheese for this dish, as it melts easily, but an aged Edam will melt almost as well and provide a much more robust flavor.

To make *Käsespätzle*, you'll want to find a device called a *Spätzlehobel*—or spätzle hopper—which resembles a cheese grater and has an attachment that allows you to move the batter through the holes and into a pot of boiling water. While spätzle hoppers are becoming more common in cookware stores, if you don't have one, you can easily make do with a flat cheese grater and a wooden spoon to push the batter through the holes. Adventurous cooks can also attempt the traditional method of making spätzle, which involves little more than a wooden board and a wide, flat metal scraper called a *Spätzlebrett und Schaber*. If all else fails, you can find frozen spätzle at some specialty grocery stores.

1. In a heavy-bottomed pan, heat butter over medium heat. Add onions and cook just until they begin to brown. Turn the heat to low and slowly caramelize the onions until they are soft, brown, and sweetly fragrant, stirring occasionally to prevent them from sticking to the pan. Add a tablespoon of water here and there if necessary to keep them from cooking too fast. When they are done, move the onions to a bowl and set the pan aside. Do not wash it.

2. In a bowl, combine the eggs and ¼ cup heavy cream and beat to mix. In another, smaller bowl, combine flour, salt, and pepper and mix well. Slowly add the dry ingredients to the wet, stirring with a wooden spoon. If the dough is too loose, add more flour a tablespoon at a time until it is the consistency of a thick batter. Cover the batter and let it rest for 20 minutes.

3. While the batter is resting, bring a large pot of water to a boil. Once it's bubbling madly, add a few tablespoons of salt and bring it back up to a boil.

4. Set your spätzle maker over the pot and press the dough through the holes into the boiling water a few inches below. If using a flat cheese grater, just press the dough through the holes with your fingers or a wooden spoon. You'll need to work in two or three batches, depending on how big your pot is. Once the spätzle float to the top, let them cook for another 2 minutes. Remove them with a slotted spoon and set them to dry on a plate lined with a paper towel. » recipe continues

5. Once all of your spätzle are done, add them to the pan that you cooked the onions in. Turn the heat to medium and cook the spätzle for 2 minutes, tossing a few times to get them to heat evenly. Add shredded cheese and 3 tablespoons of heavy cream, stirring until all the cheese is melted. Salt and pepper to taste. Serve immediately, topped with caramelized onions.

ALTERNATIVE CHEESES: Emmentaler, Raclette, any fine young Gouda, Valley Ford Highway One

WINE PAIRINGS: high-acidity, low-residual-sugar white wines such as dry or off-dry Rieslings, Alpine whites, Chardonnay, or Rhône Valley whites

ADDITIONAL PAIRINGS FOR THE CHEESE: peaches, apricots, honeydew melon, cantaloupe, cherries

SOPA SECA DE FIDEO CON TOMATILLO
Y QUESO HOJA SANTA

SERVES 4

- **12** ounces tomatillos, paper wrappers removed
- **1–2** Serrano chilies, stems removed
- **¼** medium onion
- **1** clove garlic
- **2** tablespoons chopped cilantro, plus extra for garnish
- **5** tablespoons vegetable oil, divided
- **4** ounces fresh Mexican chorizo, casing removed, crumbled
- **7** ounces capellini, broken into ½-inch pieces
- **1** teaspoon sea salt

   Freshly ground black pepper
- **2⅓** cups chicken stock
- **1** (5-ounce) round of Hoja Santa (still in its leaf wrapping), chopped and broken apart
- **1** avocado, seeded, peeled, and diced

   Crema fresca or sour cream, at room temperature

WHEN IT COMES TO MEXICAN CUISINE, THERE'S NO ONE WE TRUST MORE THAN PEG Poswall, a retired caterer and food writer living in Northern California. She's traveled through Mexico with renowned Mexican chefs, and her numerous cookbooks on the subject are stained and beaten from exuberant use. The lady knows what she's doing.

When we asked her to teach us to make a Mexican-style macaroni and cheese, she suggested we cobble together a *sopa seca de fideo*—which means, essentially, "dry soup with noodles." Traditionally, tomatoes are used to make the sauce, but we both have a fondness for the vegetal green flavors of tomatillos. The result is a quirky riff on a classic dish that is, as Peg would say, "closet good." (Meaning that you'll take the whole pot and hide in the closet so you don't have to share.)

The finishing cheese is Hoja Santa, a chèvre-style cheese crafted by Paula Lambert, an American cheese pioneer and owner of the Mozzarella Company in Dallas. The cheese is wrapped in leaves of the eponymous *hoja santa* plant, which imparts very distinct flavors of mint, licorice, and sassafras. It mingles well with the subtle taste of the tomatillos and the blazing heat of the chilies.

1. Place the tomatillos, Serrano chilies, and onion on a sheet pan and broil for about 15 minutes. They will all char and blister quite a bit. Place the broiled vegetables along with the garlic and 2 tablespoons of cilantro into a blender, being sure to fill the blender only halfway. Pulse until totally liquefied. Take care, as steam from a hot liquid can blow the top off a blender. Work in batches if necessary. Once blended, there should be about 1 cup of sauce.

2. Place 3 tablespoons of the oil in a large saucepan and set over medium heat. Add the chorizo and cook for 3 to 4 minutes or until crispy, using a wooden spoon to break up the chorizo into small crumbles. Use a slotted spoon to remove the chorizo and set aside, leaving the oil in the pan.

3. Place the broken capellini in the saucepan and return the pan to medium-high heat. Cook the noodles in the chorizo oil until well browned but not burned—it should take only a few minutes. Remove the pasta from the pan and set aside.

4. Add the remaining 2 tablespoons of oil to the pan and heat over medium-high heat. Add the tomatillo-chili puree and salt. It should bubble up violently, then quickly recede. Reduce by ¼ cup, which should take only about a minute. A wooden spoon pulled through the middle should reveal the bottom of the pan for a moment before the thick sauce covers it up.

5. Add the pasta to the sauce and cook until it absorbs the liquid. Add the chicken stock and bring to a boil, then reduce to a simmer. Allow to cook undisturbed for about 15 to 17 minutes, or until the pasta is soft and most of the liquid absorbed. The pasta will be past al dente, but you don't want to cook it into mush. It should be thick, like noodle soup but without the soup; hence the name sopa seca, "dry soup."

6. Scoop into bowls and garnish with fried chorizo, Hoja Santa, cilantro, avocado, and crema fresca or sour cream. Disappear to a closet and enjoy, or begrudgingly serve to others.

Note: *Many Mexican grocery stores carry broken capellini noodles under the name fideos cambray. Using this will save you a step in breaking up the long noodles.*

ALTERNATIVE CHEESES: Any favorite chèvre will do very nicely, but Hoja Santa's unique herbal flavor is worth seeking out.

WINE PAIRINGS: New Zealand Sauvignon Blanc, Verdejo, Vinho Verde, Txakoli, Albariño, dry California or Spanish rosé, Grenache

ADDITIONAL PAIRINGS FOR THE CHEESE: fresh figs, persimmons, apples, pears

RACLETTE WITH FARFALLE,
CORNICHONS, AND SAUTÉED ONIONS

SERVES 4

10 ounces farfalle

2 tablespoons olive oil

1 medium onion, sliced thin

16 ounces Raclette, ideally in a wheel shape (though slices or a wedge will work fine)

1 cup sliced cornichons

I RECENTLY VISITED LONDON'S BOROUGH MARKET FOR THE FIRST TIME, AND IN THIS lovely corner of the UK, I was introduced to a version of the famous dish known as raclette. Raclette, an irresistibly salty, medium-soft Swiss cheese, was melted directly under an enormous hot iron and then slathered by the pound over a mountain of French fries, cornichons, and onions. I ate many incredible things during my time wandering aimlessly around Europe, but this heavenly concoction was one of the highlights of my trip.

We tried to capture the personality of this raclette in a macaroni and cheese and found that the combination of cornichons and creamy, salty cheese takes to pasta with an addictive grace. You can also replace the pasta with French fries or other potato-based finger foods.   —SS

1. Cook the pasta in a large pot of salted boiling water until al dente. Drain through a colander and set aside.

2. Heat olive oil in a pan over medium heat. Sauté onions until they are soft and lightly browned, about 8 minutes. Heap pasta into 4 bowls and top with onions.

3. Fire up the broiler and brush a piece of aluminum foil lightly with oil. Put cheese, rind side down, on foil and place directly under heating element. As soon as the cheese has bubbled and melted, which should take about 2 minutes, tip it over a bowl of pasta and scrape a quarter of the cheese off; repeat for the other 3 bowls of pasta. Sprinkle with cornichons and serve; eat immediately, as the cheese cools off quickly.

ALTERNATIVE CHEESES: Spring Hill Reading, Sequatchie Cove Raclette, any noble Raclette or Swiss cheese

WINE PAIRINGS: off-dry Chenin Blanc, off-dry Riesling

ADDITIONAL PAIRINGS FOR THE CHEESE: stone-ground mustard, potatoes, cornichons, caramelized onions

PAN-FRIED MORBIER
MACARONI AND CHEESE

SERVES 6 TO 8

16 ounces elbow macaroni

2½ tablespoons butter, divided

¼ medium onion, chopped

2 ounces thick-cut speck, fatty bacon, salt pork, or prosciutto, finely diced

2 cups whole milk

3 tablespoons flour

¼ teaspoon sea salt

2 bay leaves

4 cloves

5 ounces Morbier, grated, rind discarded

5 ounces Fontina, grated

Panko breadcrumbs

Safflower, olive, or vegetable oil for frying

MORBIER IS A CLASSIC FRENCH CHEESE KNOWN FOR ITS MEATY, MUSHROOMY, SLIGHTLY alkaline flavor and its characteristic line of vegetable ash. The ash came about when ancient cheesemakers, left with only a bit of milk from the afternoon's milking, covered the half-filled cheese mold with vegetable ash to protect the milk until they could top it off the next morning. The ash doesn't offer any flavor, but the tradition persisted and lends this cheese an especially elegant appearance.

We tried a few recipes with Morbier and bay leaves, and while the combination was wonderfully sophisticated—worthy of bone china and pearls at the table—we still felt it could be teased into something quirky and unique. We discovered this method of pan-frying macaroni and cheese from the good people at Point Reyes creamery, who produce Point Reyes Original Blue (page 106) and Toma (page 84). Here, macaroni and cheese is made on the stove, then pressed into a baking dish and allowed to chill. The mac firms up and is then cut into squares, coated in panko, and fried in a skillet. Elegant yet homey. We find that with a light salad and a glass of chilled white wine, it makes for a delightful rainy-day lunch.

1. Cook the pasta in a large pot of salted boiling water until al dente. Drain through a colander and set aside.

2. Heat 1 tablespoon of the butter in a sauté pan over medium-low heat. Add the onions and cook for 10 to 15 minutes, stirring occasionally, until the onions are very soft and have taken on a nice golden color. Remove the onions from pan and set aside.

3. Place the speck in the sauté pan over medium-high heat and cook for 2 minutes, or until seared on all sides. If it sticks, add a teaspoon of olive oil to the pan to keep it from sticking further. The speck may smoke a bit, which is fine. Remove from pan and set aside.

4. To prepare the mornay sauce, heat the milk in a small saucepan over medium heat. As soon as the milk starts to steam and tiny bubbles form around the edges of the pan, turn off the heat. Place the remaining 1½ tablespoons of butter in a medium saucepan and melt over medium flame. Add the flour and stir with a flat-edge wooden paddle just until the roux begins to take on a light brown color, scraping the bottom to prevent burning, about 3 minutes. Stir in salt, bay leaves, and cloves. Slowly add the milk and stir constantly until the sauce thickens enough to evenly coat the back of a spoon—a finger drawn along the back of the spoon should leave a clear swath. Remove from heat and use a slotted spoon to strain out the bay leaves and cloves. Add cheese to sauce, stirring until completely melted. The sauce will be extremely thick, and long strings of cheese should adhere to the spoon when you pull it out of the sauce. ❱❱ recipe continues

5. Add the pasta, onions, and speck, mixing together well. It will be very thick and stringy, resembling the webs of marshmallow that stick to the pot when you make Rice Krispies Treats.

6. At this point, if you want, you can simply eat the recipe as is. It's pretty darn wonderful. To move on and pan-fry it, use a wooden spoon and scrape the macaroni and cheese into a 9-by-13-inch baking dish. Using an offset spatula or similar tool, flatten the top and lightly press down on the pasta to compact it. Cover with plastic wrap and press down lightly to get any air bubbles out. You may need to lift the plastic wrap to force some of the air out. Refrigerate until very solid—4 hours at least, but overnight is ideal.

7. When the macaroni is completely chilled, cut it into 12 equal rectangles. Dredge each rectangle in panko breadcrumbs, making sure to handle them lightly as you go. To fry, place 1 tablespoon of oil in a sauté pan and melt over medium-high heat. Cook 4 or 5 rectangles at a time, making sure not to crowd the pan. Fry the rectangles on both sides until nicely crispy and golden brown, flipping them over with a spatula as each side cooks. It should take about 2 to 4 minutes for each side, but use your judgment. It helps to make a test rectangle to get a feel for the frying before doing the others—you may find you need to adjust the heat or cooking time to satisfy your stovetop's quirks, or add a bit more oil after a few rectangles have been fried. Be patient. Cooking too quickly will result in a cool interior, while cooking too slowly will cause it to fall apart. Serve immediately.

ALTERNATIVE CHEESES: Fontina, Appenzeller, Gruyère, Point Reyes Toma

WINE PAIRINGS: Most unoaked white wines or sparklings, but an Alto Adige white from where speck originates would be wonderful, like a Müller-Thurgau, Pinot Bianco, Sauvignon Blanc.

ADDITIONAL PAIRINGS FOR THE CHEESE: hard, dry salamis; soft scrambled eggs; potato gratin

HONEY BZZZ WITH SCALLIONS,
ARTICHOKE HEARTS, AND SHELL PASTA

SERVES 4

- **16** ounces medium shell pasta
- **2** tablespoons olive oil
- **4** scallions, roots removed, chopped from end to end
- **1** cup coarsely chopped canned artichoke hearts
- **2¼** cups milk
- **3** tablespoons butter
- **3** tablespoons flour
- **12** ounces Honey Bzzz, rind removed, shredded
- Sea salt
- Freshly ground black pepper
- Chopped scallion greens for garnish

HOLLANDSE'S HONEY BZZZ CHÈVRE MAY WARM THE HEART OF EVEN THE MOST STUBBORN goat's-milk naysayer. Buoyantly tart with a sweet follow-up, this cheese imparts a smooch of honey one second and a big, sloppy kiss of salt the next. It is a unique cheese that will keep you captivated and begging for a second (and third, and fourth) bite.

You might not normally think of artichoke hearts in a macaroni-and-cheese dish, but when paired with Honey Bzzz's charismatic personality, they offer a tender tooth and a comforting note of green. A perfect cool evening supper for when you want to relax on the porch swing with a big bowl of cheesy goodness in your lap.

1. Cook the pasta in a large pot of salted boiling water until al dente. Drain through a colander and set aside.

2. In a sauté pan, heat oil over medium heat. Cook scallions until they just begin to change color, about 3 minutes, stirring constantly. Add artichoke hearts and cook for another 2 minutes, again stirring constantly. Remove from heat and set aside.

3. To prepare the mornay sauce, heat the milk in a small saucepan over medium heat. As soon as the milk starts to steam and tiny bubbles form around the edges of the pan, turn off the heat. Place the butter in a medium saucepan and melt over medium flame. Add the flour and stir with a flat-edge wooden paddle just until the roux begins to take on a light brown color, scraping the bottom to prevent burning, about 3 minutes. Slowly add the milk and stir constantly until the sauce thickens enough to evenly coat the back of a spoon—a finger drawn along the back of the spoon should leave a clear swath. Remove from heat and add cheese to sauce, stirring until completely melted.

4. Stir in scallions and artichoke hearts, continuing to cook for another minute. Salt and pepper to taste. Garnish with freshly chopped scallion greens and serve hot.

ALTERNATIVE CHEESES: Barely Buzzed, Midnight Moon, Keen's Cheddar, Beecher's Cheddar

WINE PAIRINGS: Tocai Friulano, Grüner Veltliner

ADDITIONAL PAIRINGS FOR THE CHEESE: chipotle, fig jam, honey

RAW-MILK CHEESE IN THE UNITED STATES

IT'S A SAD FACT THAT SOME OF THE WORLD'S most sought-after cheeses, such as true Camembert, cannot be imported to the United States. American cheesemakers are equally limited when it comes to producing raw-milk cheeses, even within their own communities. Why? you ask. Bacteria.

If you raised an eyebrow and asked: "Wait, aren't bacteria the very things that turn milk into cheese? Aren't bacteria a big part of what produces the wondrous flavors and textures craved by people around the world? Aren't bacteria supposed to be there?" Well, yes. You'd be right on all counts.

Pasteurization, the process of heating a liquid to kill potentially harmful microorganisms, has become a regular practice in American cheese production. The law stipulates that milk used to make cheese must be heated to a certain temperature for a certain amount of time (to 143°F for 30 minutes; to 161°F for 15 seconds; or to 350°F for a fraction of a second, a process called flash-heating).

The reasoning behind these regulations is that raw-milk products can make you very, very sick. But while there are indeed some famously vicious bacteria that colonize raw milk, such as listeria, salmonella, and *E. coli*, the truth is that microorganisms make the very thing we love: curdled, fermented milk, otherwise known as cheese. Pasteurization also kills the good bacteria that contribute to flavor, reflect the milk's natural terroir, and, ironically, protect the cheese from deterioration. When eaten in cheeses that have been prepared responsibly, bacteria are your friends.

This isn't to say pasteurized cheeses taste bad; in fact, you'll find countless wonderful cheeses that are made with pasteurized milk. However, raw-milk cheeses often have more depth of character and a more tantalizing mouthfeel. Remember: Raw milk generally isn't dangerous. Poor handling and unsanitary conditions are. Pasteurized milk can be just as harmful as milk that hasn't been treated to kill bacteria if it has been mishandled, since human error is the primary issue.

Now, you may be thinking, *My local cheesemonger recently sold me raw-milk cheese. Is he a criminal, harboring culinary contraband?* Not likely. You can sell some raw cheeses in the United States, but it must be aged for sixty days. The problem is, in cheese years, two months is a very long time. Much can change in a cheese's body from week to week, even day to day. An extra thirty days in the aging process makes for a very different product when it comes to nuances of color, texture, flavor, and smell.

What if you're traveling abroad? Should you follow the FDA's recommendation not to consume young raw-milk cheeses? Our stance is this: The French have been eating raw-milk cheeses for centuries, to very little ill effect. A milk's age isn't the weakest link; poor handling and unhygienic conditions are. If you're in good general health and interested in eating raw dairy products, ask around to see what producers are the most reputable. Local cheese lovers and anyone manning a quality cheese shop will be able to point you in the right direction.

BEEF STROGANOFF WITH
EGG NOODLES AND MOODY BLUE

6 tablespoons butter, divided

1½ pounds sirloin, cut into thin strips

Sea salt

Freshly ground black pepper

1 cup diced shallots (2 whole bulbs)

8 ounces cremini or button mushrooms, thinly sliced

¼ teaspoon smoked paprika

2 teaspoons fresh tarragon leaves, minced

10 ounces wide egg noodles

1 cup sour cream

1 tablespoon milk

1 tablespoon Dijon mustard

6 ounces Moody Blue, crumbled and at room temperature

ALTERNATIVE CHEESES: Smokey Blue, Smoked Ba Ba Blue, Blue Haze

WINE PAIRINGS: off-dry Riesling, Chenin Blanc, Pinot Noir

ADDITIONAL PAIRINGS FOR THE CHEESE: dried figs, Medjool dates

MOODY BLUE, A BLUE CHEESE SMOKED OVER THE WOOD OF FRUIT TREES, IS SMOKIER than most cheeses you'll find at your local cheese counter. The taste is reminiscent of an idyllic childhood filled with family campfires, slabs of sizzling bacon, and small pots of cream at breakfast. It's these flavors that make Moody Blue such a delightful addition to that Russian-American classic, beef Stroganoff.

Full of butter, mustard, sour cream, and blue cheese, our Stroganoff is a stout, creamy dream of a dish. Tarragon lends its signature green notes to the sauce, while smoked paprika ups the ante with a touch more smoky goodness. We recommend using a flavorful, high-quality beef to round out this superb example of comfort-food indulgence.

1. Place 3 tablespoons of the butter into a wide, thick-bottomed pan and set over medium-high heat. Season both sides of sirloin strips with salt and pepper. Sear beef on both sides, being careful not to burn the butter. You may have to work in batches. When the beef is done, set it aside in a large bowl.

2. Add the shallots to the pan. Reduce the heat to medium and cook for 2 minutes. Remove from heat and place the shallots in the bowl with the beef. Bring a pot of salted water to boil for the pasta.

3. While the water heats, add the remaining butter to the pan and raise heat to medium-high. Add the mushrooms and cook for 1 minute. Add the smoked paprika and tarragon and cook for another 2 to 3 minutes, or until the mushrooms are softened and browned. Remove mushrooms and place in the same bowl with the beef and shallots. Don't wash the pan and don't toss out the liquid that the mushrooms leave behind! You'll be using the pan again, and the liquid is crazy tasty and will make the sauce awesome.

4. Add the egg noodles to the boiling water. Cook until just al dente. Drain through a colander and add to the bowl with the beef and mushrooms.

5. Return the pan you used for the mushrooms to low heat. Add the sour cream, milk, Dijon mustard, and Moody Blue. Stir to incorporate the ingredients, being careful not to boil or simmer the sauce, as this will cause the sour cream to curdle. The sauce is done when the cheese is almost completely melted. Season with salt and pepper to taste.

6. Pour sauce into the bowl with the beef, noodles, shallots, and mushrooms. Toss together and serve.

SZECHUAN-STYLE UDON
WITH PIAVE AND RADICCHIO

SERVES 4

- **7** ounces udon noodles
- **1½** tablespoons sesame oil, divided
- **4** cloves garlic, finely minced
- **1** tablespoon peeled and grated ginger
- **1** teaspoon crushed, dried red pepper flakes (preferably Chinese variety, like Tien Tsin)
- **½** teaspoon Szechuan peppercorns, crushed
- **1½** cups radicchio, cut into ½-inch slices

  Sea salt

  Freshly ground black pepper
- **6** ounces Piave, finely grated

SOMEWHERE THERE'S A READER WHO IS LOOKING AT THE TITLE OF THIS RECIPE AND shrieking in disbelief. This reader is probably cursing a world that produced what might be seen as a culinary abomination. Chinese ingredients and flavors blended with cheese? Practically heresy.

Yet you'd be surprised how well these flavors meld. Piave, an Italian favorite, is creamy and full-bodied with a spicy aroma that contrasts well with the aggressive flavors of garlic, ginger, chilies, and Szechuan peppercorns. When it comes out of the wok, this surprisingly tasty multinational dish will leave any doubters in awe.

1. Cook udon noodles according to directions on the package, usually 4 minutes in boiling water and then drained in a colander. Set aside.

2. Place 1 tablespoon of sesame oil in a wok or large sauté pan over medium-high heat. Once the oil is hot and shimmering, add the garlic, ginger, red pepper flakes, and Szechuan peppercorns. Sauté for about 30 seconds, or until fragrant and toasty, stirring occasionally so as not to burn the spices.

3. Add the radicchio and sauté until slightly wilted, about 2 minutes. Add the cooked udon and the rest of the sesame oil and toss together. Salt and pepper to taste. Portion out onto plates and top each serving with grated Piave. Drizzle with more sesame oil and garnish with more Piave if desired.

Note: *You may have to order the Szechuan peppercorns online, as they're still relatively new to the United States. They have a citrusy flavor, and they produce, instead of heat, a slight numbing quality on the tongue, similar to the tingle from carbonated water. Use them judiciously.*

ALTERNATIVE CHEESES: Parmesan, Pecorino Romano

WINE PAIRINGS: Grechetto, Zinfandel

ADDITIONAL PAIRINGS FOR THE CHEESE: asparagus, buckwheat, potatoes

PANEER KORMA WITH
IDIYAPPAM NOODLES

SERVES 4 TO 6

- ½ cup vegetable oil, divided
- 1 cup paneer, cut into ½-inch cubes (for recipe, see page 23)
- ¼ cup desiccated unsweetened coconut
- 2 tablespoons coconut milk
- ¼ cup ground cashews
- 2 fresh green chilies, cut in half lengthwise
- 10 to 12 curry leaves (optional)
- 1 large onion, chopped
- 1 teaspoon sea salt
- 1 teaspoon minced ginger
- 1 teaspoon minced garlic
- ¼ teaspoon dried turmeric
- 1 teaspoon red chili flakes
- 1 tablespoon dried coriander
- 1 carrot, peeled and chopped
- 1 medium potato, peeled and cut into 1-inch cubes
- ¼ cup fresh or frozen peas
- 1 large tomato, peeled and chopped
- 2 cups water, divided
- ¼ cup chopped fresh cilantro
- ½ teaspoon garam masala
- 12 ounces idiyappam noodles, cooked

WHEN WE STARTED WRITING THIS COOKBOOK, WE CONSIDERED HOW BROADLY WE wanted to define the term *macaroni and cheese*. Surely not all noodle-and-cheese dishes were members of the club, right? But the more recipes we developed, the more our attention turned to the global community; we were surprised to learn that many cultures had much to add to our mac-and-cheese education.

The recipe below was shared with us by our good friend Vijitha Shyam, a food writer and Indian cooking teacher in San Jose, California. Vijitha has taught us more about the use of cheese in Indian food than we ever thought possible and helped to expand our view of the classic dish we've covered so deeply in this book. Really, who are we to say that another culture's version doesn't fit the bill? Wasn't the whole point of this project to think outside the (blue) box?

This dreamy dish showcases paneer cheese and idiyappam rice noodles smothered with a creamy coconut curry sauce. While it's not terribly spicy as is, you can nonetheless decrease the heat even more by omitting one of the chilies or leaving them whole instead of slicing them in half, which will prevent the seeds from lending too much of their fiery personality. This recipe is best served piping hot, with *naan*—an Indian flatbread—on the side.

1. Heat 2 tablespoons vegetable oil in a nonstick saucepan over medium heat. Add the paneer, making sure there's plenty of room to breathe between the cubes of cheese—cook in batches if you must. Fry for 3 to 5 minutes on each side, until all surfaces are gently browned. Remove with a slotted spoon and let rest on a plate lined with a paper towel. Set aside.

2. Using a small food processor (or a mortar and pestle), make a smooth paste with the coconut, coconut milk, and ground cashews. Set aside.

3. Heat remaining vegetable oil in a shallow pan. Once the oil shimmers, add green chilies and curry leaves. Allow them to cook for 1 minute, just enough to perfume the oil. Remove the curry leaves but leave the chilies, and add onions and salt. Cook for 4 minutes, stirring occasionally, allowing the onions to sweat. Cover and cook for another 8 minutes, or just until the onions brown. Do not let them burn.

4. Add ginger and garlic. Sauté for 2 minutes, until the raw smell disappears. Sprinkle in turmeric, chili flakes, and coriander, and cook for another 3 to 4 minutes.

5. Add the carrots, potatoes, and peas, stir to coat with spices, and cook for 3 minutes. Add the tomatoes and the coconut paste you made earlier and cook for another 3 minutes. Add 1 cup water, just enough to barely cover the vegetables. Cover and cook for 20 minutes, until the vegetables are cooked through. » recipe continues

6. Once you see the oil separating around the edges of the pan, gently stir in paneer cubes and cilantro. Sprinkle the top of the dish with garam masala and stir to combine. Add the remaining cup of water and mix well to combine. Simmer for 5 minutes and remove from heat. Serve hot, poured over idiyappam rice noodles.

Note: *Idiyappam noodles can be found frozen in many Indian grocery stores. They're easy enough to prepare: just thaw them out and steam according to the package directions for a light, rice-like texture. You can also make idiyappam noodles at home, though you'll need a sevai press, a handheld extruder that you can find at Indian groceries. If you can't find frozen idiyappam, use any thin Asian noodles, such as plain ramen (not the instant kind!).*

IDIYAPPAM NOODLES

18 ounces (about 500 grams) ready-made rice flour (idiyappam powder, available from Indian grocery stores)

1 teaspoon sea salt

4 cups water (more or less)

Special equipment:

Sevai noodle press

1. Sift the flour and salt twice. Set aside in a bowl.

2. Heat water in a small saucepan. Once the water comes to a boil, slowly drizzle half into the bowl of flour, mixing well with a spatula. Add more water little by little and knead to a soft dough. The amount of water varies depending on the brand of flour you use. You want the dough to be soft but not sticky.

3. Lightly grease the noodle press and add about ½ cup of dough to the chamber. Press the noodles out to form a circular mound in a steamer. Steam for about 10 minutes, until the noodles are cooked through.

BIANCO SARDO WITH COLLARD
GREENS PESTO OVER PENNE

SERVES 6

4	ounces (1 small bunch) collard greens, roughly chopped
4	ounces pecans
2	cloves garlic, chopped
7	ounces Bianco Sardo, finely grated, divided
½	teaspoon sea salt
¼	teaspoon freshly ground black pepper
¼	cup olive oil
16	ounces penne rigate

BIANCO SARDO IS A SHEEP'S-MILK CHEESE FROM ITALY THAT'S SOMEWHAT NUTTY, quite sheepy (of course), and with a grassiness that makes it distinct from other hard sheep cheeses. It's these qualities that make it pesto perfect. The pesto recipe we've included here is as unusual as the cheese itself, in that it uses collard greens instead of basil. The coarse bitterness of collards creates a delightfully rustic flavor that complements the cheese's Old World aura. We highly recommend serving this dish alongside poached salmon or grilled chicken for a relaxed meal, perfect for sharing with friends.

Feel free to use chard or kale in place of collard greens, or to add a bit of parsley or basil if you prefer. Any greens you have on hand will pair well with this cheese.

1. Place the collard greens, pecans, garlic cloves, 4 ounces of the Bianco Sardo, salt, and pepper in a food processor. Pulse on high speed while slowly trickling in the olive oil. Taste as you go and adjust the oil, salt, and pepper as needed. The pesto should be pleasantly fresh, cheesy, and somewhat bitter.

2. Cook the pasta in a large pot of salted boiling water until al dente. Drain through a colander and set aside.

3. Toss pasta with pesto. If you experience a sudden urge to drizzle in a bit more olive oil, then by all means give in to it. Top with the remaining cheese and serve.

ALTERNATIVE CHEESES: Fiore Sardo, Zamorano, Pecorino Romano, Paški Sir, or any other hard sheep's-milk cheese

WINE PAIRINGS: dry Riesling, Sauvignon Blanc

ADDITIONAL PAIRINGS FOR THE CHEESE: fava beans, fresh oregano, bitter olive oil, spinach

POINT REYES ORIGINAL BLUE
WITH PECANS, FIGS, AND SHELL PASTA

SERVES 2 AS AN ENTRÉE,
4 AS A SIDE

½ cup pecans

3 tablespoons butter

12 ounces whole wheat
shell pasta

4 ounces Point Reyes Original
Blue, coarsely crumbled

¾ cup chopped mission figs

Sea salt

Freshly ground black pepper

I WAS INTRODUCED TO POINT REYES ORIGINAL BLUE BY MY FRIEND ASHLEY TEPLIN, who insisted I try it paired with figs, walnuts, and port. At the time, I wasn't a fan of blue cheese, and I was hesitant. (I was twenty-four and naive, what can I say?) The creamy texture and fruity flavor of Point Reyes Original set me squarely on the path of blue, and I have never looked back.

Simple pairing in a no-fuss mac-and-cheese dish really allows Point Reyes to shine. The goal here isn't to cook the cheese but to apply just enough heat to melt it gently into the folds of the hot pasta. After that, a quick stir with some brown butter, figs, and toasted pecans forms a dish that's perfect by itself and also makes a great side to a finely grilled steak. I insist you indulge in a glass of port too.

In the winter, when fresh figs aren't available, I use Medjool dates. Their brown-sugary flavor is a perfect sweetener to contrast with the cheese.   —GM

1. Place the pecans in a single layer on a baking sheet. Roast in a 350°F oven for 7 minutes. Set aside to cool. Once they're cooled, chop the pecans coarsely.

2. Heat a heavy-bottomed skillet over medium heat. Add the butter and cook. The butter will foam and then subside. Eventually, lightly browned specks will form on the bottom of the pan. The butter will turn a light brown and begin to smell nutty. Be sure to keep an eye on it, as it can go from brown to black in an instant. Remove from the heat immediately and pour into a bowl.

3. Cook the pasta in a large pot of salted boiling water until al dente. Drain through a colander. Place back in the pot with the heat still on. Combine the noodles with the brown butter and Point Reyes Original Blue and gently toss until the cheese has softened and melted a little. Add the pecans and figs and continue tossing. Add salt and pepper to taste and serve.

ALTERNATIVE CHEESES: Shaft's Blue, Gorgonzola, Bayley Hazen Blue

WINE PAIRINGS: Grenache Blanc, champagne, port

ADDITIONAL PAIRINGS FOR THE CHEESE: local honey, roasted apricots, roasted nectarines, fresh green grapes, dates

SWISS CHARD, ROTINI,
AND CANNELLINI BEANS
IN PARMESAN BROTH

SERVES 6 TO 8

- 1 tablespoon olive oil
- 3 cloves garlic, minced
- ½ cup minced shallots (1 whole bulb)
- ¼ teaspoon chili flakes
- 8 cups chicken stock
- 1 sprig thyme
- 8 ounces Parmesan rinds
- 4 ounces rotini or fusilli
- 5 ounces Swiss chard, stemmed and cut into 1-inch ribbons
- 2 (15-ounce) cans cannellini beans, rinsed
- Zest of 1 lemon
- Sea salt
- Freshly ground black pepper
- Juice of 1 lemon
- 2 to 4 ounces Parmesan, finely grated

ALL TOO OFTEN, PEOPLE TOSS AWAY THE RINDS FROM THEIR PARMESAN, NOT REALIZING what flavorful bounty they are. Just like the greens from leeks or the bones of a chicken, these scraps have tons of flavor if you know how to coax it out. Stuff a chicken with Parmesan rinds before roasting; toast them under a broiler and use them as Parmesan "croutons"; or pop them into a pot and simmer them to make a hypnotic Parmesan broth.

This aromatic brew is sure to lure anyone nearby into the kitchen. The flavor is salty, nutty, and unmistakably cheesy. Fortified with a bit of pasta, hearty Swiss chard, and cannellini beans, it results in a soup that is satisfying, inexpensive, and easy to make.

1. Place olive oil in a large pot and heat over medium-high heat. Add the garlic, shallots, and chili flakes, and stir until the shallots are translucent and the garlic takes on a bit of color. Add the stock, thyme, and Parmesan rinds. Bring to a boil over high heat, then reduce the heat to low. Cover the soup and simmer for 30 minutes, being sure to scrape the bits of cheese from the bottom of the pot every few minutes with a wooden spoon. Feel free to eat the melty bits that stick to the spoon.

2. Turn heat to medium and bring back to a boil. Add the pasta and cook until al dente. Remove the remaining Parmesan rinds and discard (or nibble them, suck on them, give them to the dog). Add the Swiss chard and beans. Cover and allow to simmer for 10 more minutes.

3. Stir the lemon zest into the soup and add salt and pepper to taste. Serve in bowls and garnish each with a fresh spritz of lemon juice and a fine dusting of the grated Parmesan.

Note: *Parmesan rinds can be purchased at many stores that sell fine cheese, but if you have rinds at home, store them in a plastic zip-top bag in the freezer until ready to use.*

WINE PAIRINGS: Canary Islands whites, unoaked Slovenian whites, Italian Cortese

HEARTY AND SATISFYING

CHAPTER 4:
HEARTY AND SATISFYING

For many,

the best macaroni-and-cheese casserole is simply elbow macaroni drowning in a creamy cheese sauce, loaded with Cheddar, and topped with a crispy, golden crust of breadcrumbs. In reality, it can be so much more than that. There's a reason that most people consider macaroni and cheese the quintessential comfort food. It's what we eat on cold winter nights, it's what we made to impress first dates in college, and it's what we dig into when we've had a miserable day and want nothing more than a soft, warm cheesy blanket.

We consider the recipes in this chapter hearty and satisfying for a reason: cheese and pasta baked together create epic experiences in texture and flavor. We take the mundane, everyday macaroni-and-cheese casserole to the next level by drawing inspiration from numerous unique cheeses. Fatty guanciale is paired with a mellow Shaft's Blue Cheese; a brusque, porter-laden Cheddar cooks up chocolaty and bold; a robust pastitsio achieves perfection when slathered with a rich meat sauce and a salty kefalotyri topping. These dishes will assuage even the most profound macaroni-and-cheese ennui.

When making a macaroni casserole, do not overbake, or your once-lustrous sauce will become too thick and chunky, losing that characteristic mouthfeel we look for in this dish. Similarly, remember to slightly undercook the noodles in these recipes, since pasta will continue to absorb moisture in the oven surrounded by all that sauce and cheese. Take a bite of the pasta as it approaches the appropriate level of doneness. It should be just al dente, or slightly firm and toothsome. When it comes to pre-cooking pasta for a baked casserole, it's better to err on the side of under- rather than overcooked noodles, lest you end up with a mushy (though still delicious) dish.

LINCOLNSHIRE POACHER WITH
COTIJA, CHORIZO, AND PENNE

SERVES 4 TO 6

½ pound (2 large links) fresh Mexican chorizo

1 teaspoon olive oil

12 ounces penne rigate

4 ounces Cotija, shredded

1½ cups whole milk

2 tablespoons butter

2 tablespoons flour

½ teaspoon ground chipotle peppers

⅛ teaspoon cumin

1 pound, 2 ounces Lincolnshire Poacher, shredded, divided

Sea salt

Freshly ground black pepper

Two scallions, green parts only, minced

ALTERNATIVE CHEESES: Montgomery's Cheddar, Avalanche's Clothbound Goat Cheddar, Fiscalini Bandage Wrapped Cheddar, or any hard, well-aged Cheddar

WINE PAIRINGS: Grenache, Syrah, a good Rhône Valley red blend, European or domestic Sauvignon Blanc, dry Riesling

ADDITIONAL PAIRINGS FOR THE CHEESE: chutney, salami, apples

PERHAPS IT'S RARE TO FIND ENGLAND AND MEXICO SHARING COMMON GROUND IN THE culinary world, but this dish is a delightful exception. Fiery chorizo is balanced unusually well by Lincolnshire Poacher's mellow, complex, and slightly grassy flavors. This cheese, produced by Simon and Tim Jones at their farm at Ulceby Grange, adjacent to the Lincolnshire Wolds in England, is a particular favorite among milder Cheddars. We've added a touch of salty Cotija, a hard cow's-milk cheese that's named after a town in Michoacán, Mexico. Cotija is moist, granular, and delightfully salty, so be sure not to oversalt your mornay sauce.

1. Squeeze the chorizos out of their casings and break into bite-size pieces. Place the olive oil in a pan over medium heat and cook the chorizo until well browned, about 10 minutes. Transfer to a plate lined with a paper towel to drain the excess grease.

2. Cook the pasta in salted boiling water until al dente. Drain through a colander and set aside.

3. Preheat the oven to 350°F. Lightly butter a 9-inch-square or similar-sized baking dish. Toss together the pasta, chorizo, and Cotija in the baking dish.

4. To prepare the mornay sauce, heat the milk in a small saucepan over medium heat. As soon as the milk starts to steam and tiny bubbles form around the edges of the pan, turn off the heat. Place the butter in a medium saucepan and melt over medium flame. Add the flour and stir with a flat-edge wooden paddle just until the roux begins to take on a light brown color, scraping the bottom to prevent burning, about 3 minutes. Slowly add the milk, chipotle peppers, and cumin, stirring constantly until the sauce thickens enough to evenly coat the back of a spoon—a finger drawn along the back of the spoon should leave a clear swath. Remove from heat and add most of the Lincolnshire Poacher to the sauce—reserve a handful or so for topping— and stir until completely melted. Season with salt and pepper to taste. Be careful with the salt, as the cheese is already salty.

5. Pour sauce over the pasta. Top with the reserved Cheddar and green scallions. Bake for 25 minutes. Allow the dish to cool for 5 minutes before serving, then garnish with a bit more freshly chopped scallion if desired.

RED HAWK MACARONI WITH
PROSCIUTTO AND RASPBERRY JAM

SERVES 4

- **8** ounces elbow macaroni
- **1** full wheel Red Hawk, rind intact, chopped into chunks
- **4** thin slices prosciutto, chopped
- **1** teaspoon sea salt
  Freshly ground black pepper
- **2** cups heavy cream
- **4** tablespoons raspberry jam (plus more per your indulgence)

RED HAWK, PERHAPS THE MOST POPULAR CHEESE MADE BY CALIFORNIA'S COWGIRL Creamery, is a mellow and complex washed-rind cheese. While it deserves its moment in the spotlight, it doesn't fare well with complicated pairings; rather, this triple-cream appreciates a modest presentation that allows its pungent, meaty notes to speak for themselves.

For this dish, we decided to let Red Hawk's heartiness take center stage, accompanied by only a bit of salty prosciutto and a touch of tart jam. You'll be surprised how these two ingredients accentuate what makes Red Hawk so beloved—an understated intensity that puts it at the top of many cheese lovers' top 10 lists.

1. Preheat oven to 350°F.

2. Cook pasta in a large pot of salted boiling water until al dente. Drain through a colander and set aside.

3. In a large bowl, mix pasta, cheese, and prosciutto. Sprinkle with salt and a few good turns of the pepper grinder. Toss until well combined.

4. Lightly oil four 8-ounce ramekins and fill them with equal amounts of the pasta, cheese, and prosciutto mixture. Add a scant ½ cup of cream to each ramekin.

5. Line a rimmed baking sheet with foil and place your ramekins onto the sheet. Slide into oven and bake for 35 minutes, or until the cream has thickened into a nice gratin. Remove from oven and allow to sit for 10 minutes. The cheese is supposed to bubble over the edges of the ramekins—that's part of the charm of this dish. And it's why you lined the baking sheet with foil.

6. Top each ramekin with 1 tablespoon raspberry jam before serving. Add more spoonfuls of jammy goodness if you see fit.

ALTERNATIVE CHEESES: Époisses, Langres

WINE PAIRINGS: domestic Pinot Noir, sparkling rosé, champagne

ADDITIONAL PAIRINGS FOR THE CHEESE: honey, panforte, dried apricots

PASTITSIO WITH KEFALOTYRI
AND LAMB

SERVES 4 TO 6

For the meat sauce:

- 2   tablespoons olive oil
- 1¼ pounds ground lamb
- 1   small onion, diced
- 2   cloves garlic, minced
- 1   (14-ounce) can crushed tomatoes
- 4   tablespoons tomato paste
- ½   cup dry white wine
- ½   teaspoon cinnamon
- ¼   teaspoon allspice
- 1   teaspoon chopped fresh oregano leaves
- ¼   teaspoon chopped fresh rosemary leaves
- 1   large bay leaf, or 2 small bay leaves
- ½   teaspoon sea salt
- ¼   teaspoon freshly ground black pepper

For the pasta:

- 2   eggs, divided
- 12 ounces bucatini or penne
- 1   teaspoon olive oil
- 4   ounces kefalotyri, grated
     Sea salt and freshly ground black pepper

For the mornay sauce:

- 3   cups whole milk
- 3   tablespoons butter
- 3   tablespoons flour
- 10 ounces kefalotyri, grated, divided
- ¼   teaspoon sea salt
- ¼   teaspoon freshly ground black pepper

KEFALOTYRI, A FIRM GREEK CHEESE MADE OF SHEEP'S MILK—AND SOMETIMES OF A blend of sheep's and goat's milk—is so intoxicatingly salty that fans of the brine will bow down in gratitude the first time they taste it. Even those who aren't terribly addicted to salt will love kefalotyri; on the heels of this cheese's epic salinity follows the gentle sweetness of ewe's milk.

Pastitsio is one of the heartier casseroles in this book, a layering of lamb, pasta, and mornay sauce, a trifecta of Greek goodness. This is a perfect dish for winter dinner parties when you want to impress your guests with your comfort-food skills. Feel free to make this dish the day before—much like lasagna, pastitsio tastes twice as good the next day, after the flavors have had a chance to marry in the refrigerator.

You can find kefalotyri at Mediterranean markets or other international grocery stores, but Pecorino Romano makes a fine substitute in a pinch. Cheese lovers' bonus: When eaten straight off the wheel, young kefalotyri gives a satisfying squeak against the teeth.

1. In a large saucepan, heat olive oil over medium flame until it shimmers. Add lamb and cook for 5 minutes, stirring occasionally, until it is decently browned. Drain off about half the fat from the pan. Add onions and cook, stirring occasionally, until they are soft. Add garlic and cook for 1 minute, then add crushed tomatoes, tomato paste, white wine, cinnamon, allspice, oregano, rosemary, bay leaf, salt, and pepper. Stir together and reduce heat to low. Cover and simmer for 30 minutes, stirring occasionally, until most of the liquid in the sauce has been absorbed. Remove sauce from heat, remove bay leaf from sauce, and set sauce aside.

2. Crack the eggs and separate them. Place the yolks in a bowl, beat them, and set aside for use in the mornay sauce. Using a whisk or electric mixer, beat the egg whites at high speed until they are light and foamy. The whites should form soft peaks— meaning that if you pull the beaters out of the egg whites, the beaten whites should form gentle peaks that droop back into themselves.

3. While the meat sauce is simmering, prepare the noodles. Cook the pasta in a large pot of salted boiling water until *almost* al dente—you want to cook the pasta about three-quarters of the time the package recommends. Drain through a colander. If using bucatini, cut the noodles so that they fit lengthwise into an 8-by-8-inch glass baking dish without bending. Pour noodles back into the cooking pot. Add 1 teaspoon of olive oil and toss pasta until it is coated well. Let sit for 1 minute before adding the egg whites and 4 ounces of grated cheese. Toss well and season with a little salt and pepper to taste. Set aside, stirring occasionally to prevent sticking. ❯❯ recipe continues

4. Preheat oven to 350°F. While the pasta is cooking, prepare the mornay sauce. Heat the milk in a small saucepan over medium heat. As soon as the milk starts to steam and tiny bubbles form around the edges of the pan, turn off the heat. Place the butter in a medium saucepan and melt over medium flame. Add the flour and stir with a flat-edge wooden paddle just until the roux begins to take on a light brown color, scraping the bottom to prevent burning, about 3 minutes. Slowly add the milk and stir constantly until the sauce thickens enough to evenly coat the back of a spoon—a finger drawn along the back of the spoon should leave a clear swath. Remove from heat.

5. Slowly add ¼ cup of mornay sauce to the beaten egg yolks and whisk quickly. Add another ¼ cup of sauce and whisk again. Whisk the egg yolks into the larger pot of sauce. Reserve ½ cup of cheese and set it aside, and stir the rest into the sauce. Slowly stir the sauce until the cheese has melted, adding salt and pepper. Set aside.

6. Lightly grease the bottom and sides of a deep 8-by-8-inch glass baking dish or similar-size deep casserole dish with olive oil. Quickly stir the pasta and add half to the bottom of the baking dish, smoothing it out into an even layer that covers the entire bottom of the dish, the pasta lined up like straws in a box. Gently pour the meat sauce over the pasta, smooth to cover all noodles, then add the remaining pasta and smooth it out to an even layer that completely covers the meat sauce.

7. Carefully pour the mornay sauce over the pasta, again making sure every surface is covered. Sprinkle the top with the reserved cheese and slide into the oven. (Note: You may want to set the baking dish on a cookie sheet, as sauce may bubble over the sides as the casserole cooks.) Cook for 30 minutes, until the cheesy top is golden brown. Allow to cool for another 30 minutes before serving, or refrigerate overnight, reheating in a 225°F oven for 30 to 45 minutes or until bubbly.

ALTERNATIVE CHEESES: Kefalograviera, Paški Sir, Pecorino Romano

WINE PAIRINGS: Barbera, Nebbiolo, Aglianico, aged Rioja (Tempranillo)

ADDITIONAL PAIRINGS FOR THE CHEESE: grilled eggplant, pesto, grilled figs

GRANA PADANO WITH FUSILLI
AND SUN-DRIED TOMATO PESTO

SERVES 4 TO 6

8   ounces Grana Padano, finely grated, divided

1   (8-ounce) jar sun-dried tomatoes in oil

1   cup chopped walnuts

3   cloves garlic

1½ tablespoons tomato paste

½   teaspoon sea salt

¼   teaspoon freshly ground black pepper

3   tablespoons olive oil, divided

10 ounces fusilli

3   cups milk

1   tablespoon flour

ALTERNATIVE CHEESES: Parmesan, Vella Dry Jack, Spring Hill Dry Jack

WINE PAIRINGS: Tocai Friulano from Friuli, Dolcetto, Nero d'Avola, Lemberger or Blaufränkisch from Austria

ADDITIONAL PAIRINGS FOR THE CHEESE: prosciutto, speck, extra-virgin olive oil and freshly ground black pepper

ONE CAN NEVER HAVE TOO MANY PESTO RECIPES. BASIL ISN'T IN SEASON ALL YEAR round, so when you're craving a chunky, flavorful sauce that you can whip together without a thought, it's nice to have a dish like this to fall back on. And as any pesto junkie will tell you, a pesto with sun-dried tomatoes is the way to go.

The cheese most often used for tomato pesto is Grana Padano, an ancient, hard cow's-milk cheese just as dearly beloved by the Italians as Parmesan. Grana Padano is produced only in the Po River Valley under very strict guidelines, and it has been made this way for nearly a thousand years. It has a flavor similar to Parmesan, although it's smoother and milkier. It's mellow but assertive.

Grana Padano's flavor is matched perfectly with walnuts and intensely acidic sun-dried tomatoes. This pesto, delightful on its own, is swirled into a mornay and baked with pasta for a rustic macaroni and cheese. We recommend you enjoy it on the patio with a Lombardy red wine.

1. Place half of the Grana Padano, all of the sun-dried tomatoes and their oil, the walnuts, garlic cloves, tomato paste, salt, pepper, and 1 tablespoon of olive oil into the bowl of a food processor. Pulse until chopped into a slightly chunky pesto. This will make more than you will need for the recipe. Save the leftovers in an airtight container for three days; the pesto is wonderful over eggs or made into a tartine.

2. Preheat oven to 350°F. Grease an 8-by-8-inch baking dish or similar-size casserole dish with a bit of olive oil.

3. Cook the pasta in a large pot of salted boiling water until al dente. Drain through a colander and pour into a greased dish. Toss occasionally to prevent the pasta from sticking.

4. To prepare the mornay sauce, heat the milk in a small saucepan over medium heat. As soon as the milk starts to steam and tiny bubbles form around the edges of the pan, turn off the heat. Place the remaining 2 tablespoons of olive oil in a medium saucepan and heat over medium flame. Add the flour and stir with a flat-edge wooden paddle just until the roux begins to take on a light brown color, scraping the bottom to prevent burning, about 3 minutes. Slowly add the milk and stir constantly until the sauce thickens enough to evenly coat the back of a spoon—a finger drawn along the back of the spoon should leave a clear swath. Remove from heat and stir in salt and pepper to taste. Add more cheese to the sauce, reserving ¼ cup, and stir until completely melted.

5. Add 1½ cups of the pesto to the mornay sauce and quickly whisk until smooth. The sauce will be thin and slightly grainy. Pour it over the pasta and bake for 30 minutes. Allow to cool for 5 minutes before serving. Garnish with remaining Grana Padano.

SHAFT'S BLUE CHEESE WITH
GUANCIALE, BRUSSELS SPROUTS, AND PENNE

SERVES 4

- ½ cup chopped guanciale (or 4 thick strips of raw bacon, chopped)
- 1 cup quartered Brussels sprouts, stems and loose outer leaves discarded
- 7 ounces penne rigate
- 1 cup milk
- 3 tablespoons butter
- 1 tablespoon flour
- ½ teaspoon mustard powder
- ¼ teaspoon sea salt
- ¼ teaspoon freshly ground black pepper
- 8 ounces Shaft's Blue Cheese, crumbled
- ¼ cup breadcrumbs

ALTERNATIVE CHEESES: Point Reyes Blue, Faribault St. Pete's Select Blue, Oregon Blue, Gorgonzola Dolce

WINE PAIRINGS: Grüner Veltliner, Tocai Friulano

ADDITIONAL PAIRINGS FOR THE CHEESE: Medjool dates, pear preserves

SHAFT'S BLUE CHEESE EARNED ITS NAME BECAUSE IT IS AGED IN AN OLD CALIFORNIA gold mine. Though not the treasure the forty-niners were looking for, this cheese is just as rich as anything those prospectors could have found during the gold rush.

We created this recipe based on a dish we had at the Magpie Café in Sacramento. We were so impressed by the café's macaroni and cheese that we spent half the meal trying to glean exactly what was in the recipe and the following morning reverse-engineering it. This mild, sweet blue cheese is a perfect match for salty guanciale, and it tames the bitterness of sautéed Brussels sprouts.

1. Cook the guanciale over medium heat until it has released its fat and is slightly crispy. Drain the cooked bits on a paper towel and remove all but 3 tablespoons of the fat. (Feel free to save the rest for later use.) Add the Brussels sprouts to the pan, season them with a bit of salt and pepper, and sear them in the fat. The sprouts will jump around a bit as they cook. Once they've softened up slightly and turned golden brown on the cut sides, remove from the heat and set aside.

2. Cook the pasta in a large pot of salted boiling water until al dente. Drain through a colander and set aside in the dish.

3. Preheat the oven to 350°F. Lightly oil an 8-by-8-inch baking dish. Toss together the pasta, guanciale, and Brussels sprouts in the dish.

4. To prepare the mornay sauce, heat the milk in a small saucepan over medium heat. As soon as the milk starts to steam and tiny bubbles form around the edges of the pan, turn off the heat. Place the butter in a medium saucepan and melt over medium flame. Add the flour and stir with a flat-edge wooden paddle just until the roux begins to take on a light brown color, scraping the bottom to prevent burning, about 3 minutes. Slowly add the milk and stir constantly until the sauce thickens enough to evenly coat the back of a spoon—a finger drawn along the back of the spoon should leave a clear swath. Remove from heat and stir in mustard, salt, and pepper. Add cheese to sauce and stir until completely melted. Season with more salt and pepper to taste.

5. Pour sauce over the pasta. Sprinkle liberally with breadcrumbs and bake for 25 minutes. Allow the dish to cool for 5 minutes before serving.

CAMPO DE MONTALBAN
MINI-GALETTES WITH BROCCOLI AND PROSCIUTTO

SERVES 4 AS AN ENTRÉE,
8 AS A SIDE

- 1½ cups (3 sticks) plus 1 tablespoon cold butter
- 3¾ cups flour
- 1 tablespoon sugar
- ¾ teaspoon sea salt
- 16 ounces Campo de Montalban, rind removed, shredded, divided
- 6 tablespoons ice water
- 2 tablespoons olive oil
- 1 small head broccoli, chopped into tiny florets
- 8 ounces elbow macaroni
- 1 pound spicy prosciutto, chopped
- 1 egg, beaten
- 1 tablespoon water

Special equipment:

Rolling pin

CAMPO DE MONTALBAN IS A STRONG-WILLED CHEESE, ASSERTIVE AND RESOLUTE IN character. The Inigo Montoya of cheese, if you will, after he quit boozing near the end of the film. A mix of cow's, goat's, and sheep's milk, this Spanish cheese resembles a Manchego, though with its mixed-milk personality, it brings something entirely different to the table than its sheep's-milk-only cousin does.

Firm and nutty with a hint of sweetness, Campo de Montalban may seem an unlikely selection for a macaroni-and-cheese dish, but when wrapped in pastry, this cheese is raring to go. These mini-galettes are perfect for lunch; the macaroni and cheese is on the drier side, making for very little mess. They can be picked up and eaten by hand (and should be at every opportunity). This dish can be prepared up to a day ahead of time and reheated in a 200°F oven for 20 minutes, making them party perfect.

You can also enjoy this macaroni casserole without the pastry, baked in a casserole dish at 350°F for 25 minutes. In this case, we recommend topping with torn French bread and extra cheese before baking.

1. Chop butter into small chunks, cover with plastic, and set in the freezer for 5 minutes. Prepare the pie dough by combining flour, sugar, salt, and ½ cup of the shredded cheese in the bowl of a food processor. Pulse a few times to mix completely. Add the butter from the freezer and pulse until the butter lumps are each about half the size of a pea. Trickle in ice water, pulsing until the dough comes together into a ball. You may need to add another teaspoon or two of ice water. Roll dough into four round balls of equal size and flatten each gently with your hand. Wrap in plastic and chill in the refrigerator for 1 hour. The dough can be made the night before if you like.

2. Preheat oven to 375°F. Line two large baking sheets with parchment.

3. In a saucepan, heat olive oil over a medium-high heat. Sauté broccoli quickly, just until the edges are nicely browned. Remove from heat.

4. Cook the pasta in a large pot of salted boiling water until al dente. Drain thoroughly through a colander.

5. In a large bowl, toss together broccoli, cooked pasta, more cheese (reserve another 5 tablespoons for later), and prosciutto until they are well mixed.

6. Mix egg and 1 tablespoon water. Set aside.

7. Using a rolling pin, roll out the first ball of dough between two pieces of parchment until you have a circle that is about ¼ inch thick and 12 inches in diameter. Invert the pieces of parchment so that the bottom piece is now on the top. Gently peel away the top piece of parchment. ❱❱ recipe continues

If your dough circle is of an irregular shape, trim it to be mostly circular and use the removed dough to fill in any gaps to keep the filling from leaking out. Transfer the dough circle to the lined baking sheet. Repeat with each ball of dough.

8. Spoon macaroni-and-cheese filling into the middle of each dough circle, leaving a 1½-inch border around the edges of the dough. Fold the edge of the dough up over the filling, about 2 inches at a time, making sure the corner of each fold slightly overlaps the one behind it and forms a pleated effect. Use a pastry brush to lightly coat the edges of each galette with egg wash. Fill the middle opening of each pastry with 1 tablespoon or so of cheese, creating a little layer of cheese that obscures the galette filling and lightly covers the outer crust.

9. Slide the baking sheets into the oven and bake for 30 to 35 minutes, until the cheese on top of each galette is golden brown and the pastry is a nice gold color. Remove from oven and let sit for 5 minutes before serving. If you like your crust even browner, feel free to slide the galettes under the broiler for a minute once you take them out of the oven.

ALTERNATIVE CHEESES: Manchego, Gabietou

WINE PAIRINGS: Tocai Friulano or white wine from Friuli, Grüner Veltliner, Côtes du Rhône blanc

ADDITIONAL PAIRINGS FOR THE CHEESE: pickled figs or apricots, dried figs, toasted almonds

APPENZELLER CASSEROLE
WITH HAM AND KOHLRABI

SERVES 4 TO 6

6 tablespoons butter, divided

1½ cups peeled and cubed kohlrabi

½ pound chopped wet-cured ham, cut into ½-inch pieces (should be 1½ cups)

8 ounces elbow macaroni

½ teaspoon caraway seeds

¼ teaspoon celery seeds

2 cups milk

3 tablespoons flour

10 ounces Appenzeller, shredded, divided

¼ cup Parmesan, shredded

Pinch of nutmeg

Pinch of cayenne

Sea salt

Freshly ground black pepper

Chopped parsley to garnish

ALTERNATIVE CHEESES: Montagne du Jura, Heublumen, Emmentaler, Prättigauer, St. Gall

WINE PAIRINGS: Altesse, Roussette de Savoie, Pinot Noir, rosé

ADDITIONAL PAIRINGS FOR THE CHEESE: apples, pears, dried cranberries, sour cherries

KOHLRABI IS PALE GREEN, TASTES A LOT LIKE BROCCOLI STEMS, AND LOOKS LIKE Sputnik, but it's a godsend in the colder months when you're fed up with winter squash and sweet potatoes. It also makes an epic pairing with Appenzeller, a hard cheese from the Appenzell region of Switzerland. Its slight herbaceous flavor comes from the various herbs and wines in the bathing solutions that the wheels are washed in, and it makes the cheese a joy to pair in a pasta dish.

Toasted caraway and celery seeds complement the vegetal profile of Appenzeller, bringing out its unique flavors. As for the ham—well, ham just makes everything better.

1. Place 3 tablespoons of the butter in a skillet over medium heat. Once melted, add the kohlrabi and cook gently for 8 to 10 minutes. Remove from skillet and set aside. Add the ham and cook over medium heat, just until it's browned and the edges are a bit crispy. Set aside.

2. Cook the pasta in a large pot of salted boiling water until al dente. Drain through a colander and set aside.

3. Preheat the oven to 350°F. Lightly butter an 8-by-8-inch baking dish. Toss together the pasta, kohlrabi, and ham in the dish.

4. In a dry skillet over medium heat, toast the caraway seeds for 2 to 3 minutes, just until they become fragrant. Add the celery seeds and keep them moving for another minute or until they too become fragrant, being careful not to burn them. Remove from heat and set aside.

5. To prepare the mornay sauce, heat the milk in a small saucepan over medium heat. As soon as the milk starts to steam and tiny bubbles form around the edges of the pan, turn off the heat. Place the remaining 3 tablespoons of butter in a saucepan and melt over medium flame. Add the flour and stir with a flat-edge wooden paddle just until the roux begins to take on a light brown color, scraping the bottom to prevent burning, about 3 minutes. Slowly add the milk and stir constantly until the sauce thickens enough to evenly coat the back of a spoon—a finger drawn along the back of the spoon should leave a clear swath. Remove from heat and add 8 ounces of Appenzeller, all of the Parmesan, nutmeg, cayenne, caraway seeds, and celery seeds, and stir until cheese is almost completely melted. Salt and pepper to taste.

6. Pour sauce over the pasta, kohlrabi, and ham. Blanket the top with the reserved Appenzeller and bake for 25 minutes. Allow the dish to cool for 10 minutes before serving. Garnish with chopped parsley.

PUMPKIN STUFFED WITH
FONTINA, ITALIAN SAUSAGE, AND MACARONI

SERVES 4

- 1 sugar pumpkin, or other sweet variety (not a carving pumpkin), about 5 pounds

   Sea salt

   Freshly ground black pepper

- 1 tablespoon olive oil
- ¼ pound mild Italian pork sausage
- 4 ounces elbow macaroni
- 5 ounces Fontina, cut into ¼-inch cubes
- 2 ounces Gruyère, cut into ¼-inch cubes
- 3 scallions, diced
- 1 teaspoon chopped fresh rosemary
- 1 teaspoon chopped fresh thyme
- 1 teaspoon chopped fresh sage
- 1 cup heavy cream

FONTINA IS A CREAMY, WOODSY, ALPINE-STYLE CHEESE. THERE ARE MANY VARIETIES of Fontina, from Swiss to Italian, with some fine specimens even coming out of Wisconsin. Each has its own unique profile, so be sure to taste them all and pick the one that you like best. Regardless of which you choose, you will get a nice, semihard texture and subtle mushroomy flavor.

It just so happens that Fontina pairs beautifully with the sugary flavors of a good baking pumpkin. This recipe, baked inside the pumpkin—a trick inspired by Dorie Greenspan and Ruth Reichl, both famous for their stuffed-pumpkin recipes (among other things)—simply knocked our socks off with flavor and a stylish yet homey presentation.

Although best with Fontina (and a touch of Gruyère, another Alpine favorite), this recipe is flexible and can use whatever cheeses, meats, onions, or extra pasta you have on hand. Feel free to experiment.

1. Preheat the oven to 350°F. Cut a circle from the top of the pumpkin at a 45-degree angle, the way you would cut open a pumpkin to make a jack-o'-lantern, and set aside. Scoop out the seeds and strings as best you can. Generously salt and pepper the inside of the pumpkin, pop the top back on it, place it on a rimmed baking dish (since the pumpkin may leak or weep a bit), and bake for 45 minutes.

2. Meanwhile, heat the olive oil in a sauté pan over medium heat. If the sausages are in their casings, remove the meat and discard the casings. Crumble the sausage meat into small chunks and cook until lightly browned. Remove the sausage from the pan with a slotted spoon and set aside to cool. Discard the drippings, or save for gravy or what have you.

3. Also while the pumpkin bakes, cook the pasta in a large pot of salted boiling water until al dente. Drain through a colander and rinse with cool water to stop the cooking process.

4. In a bowl, toss together the Fontina, Gruyère, sausage, pasta, scallions, and herbs. Once the pumpkin is done baking, take it out of the oven and fill it with the macaroni and cheese. Pour the cream over the filling. Place the top back on the pumpkin and bake for 1 hour, taking the top off for the last 15 minutes so the cheese on top of the filling can properly brown. If the top cream still seems a bit too wobbly and liquid, give it another 10 minutes in the oven. The cream may bubble over a bit, which is fine. If the pumpkin splits while baking, as occasionally happens, be thankful you set it in a rimmed baking dish and continue to bake as normal. ❯❯ recipe continues

5. Allow the pumpkin to rest for 10 minutes before serving. Be careful moving the dish, as the pumpkin may be fragile. You can serve this dish two ways: Cut it into sections and serve them, or just scoop out the insides with scrapings of the pumpkin flesh for each serving. Either way is just dandy. Salt and pepper to taste.

ALTERNATIVE CHEESES: Fontina and Gruyère are widely available and are best used for this recipe, but feel free to try your favorite cheese. We particularly like Valley Ford's Estero Gold or its Highway 1 Fontina, as well as Roth Käse's MezzaLuna Fontina. If you want to try something radical, a creamy blue cheese like Buttermilk Blue or Cambozola will do nicely too.

WINE PAIRINGS: white Rhône Valley blends, Viognier, oaky Chardonnay, champagne

ADDITIONAL PAIRINGS FOR THE CHEESE: apples, toasted walnuts, toasted hazelnuts

DOP—WHAT IS IT?

IN CASE YOU'RE WONDERING WHAT DOP means, it's an abbreviation for the Italian term *Denominazione di Origine Protetta*, or Protected Designation of Origin. A cheese that has been awarded a DOP certification is guaranteed to originate from a very specific locality in Italy, which changes depending on the cheese in question. It also ensures that the cheese has been made and aged according to strict, often traditional, guidelines, certifying the finished product is of the very highest standard.

Some DOP cheeses you'll find in this book include Asiago, Fontina, Piave, and Taleggio.

NICASIO SQUARE AND
SPINACH-PASTA MINI-COCOTTES

SERVES 5

10 ounces spinach penne (fusilli would be fine too)

1 (10-ounce) package frozen spinach, thawed and shredded

2 cups milk

2 tablespoons butter

2 tablespoons flour

1 to 1½ heaping teaspoons chili flakes

Sea salt

Freshly ground black pepper

12 ounces Nicasio Square, rind removed, chilled and sliced thin

ALTERNATIVE CHEESES: Bachensteiner, Nicasio Reserve, Taleggio, Robiola

WINE PAIRINGS: off-dry Riesling, Gewürztraminer, Barbera red

ADDITIONAL PAIRINGS FOR THE CHEESE: caramelized onions, stone-ground mustard, pickled okra

NICASIO VALLEY CHEESE COMPANY IS ONE OF THOSE FAIRY-TALE DAIRIES YOU DREAM of: green pastures, happy cows, organic methods, and creamy milk. It was started when Fredolino Lafranchi immigrated to America from Maggia, Switzerland. In 1919, he and his wife, Zelma Dolcini Lafranchi, started the Lafranchi Dairy in Nicasio, California. These days, production is overseen by Scott Lafranchi with the assistance of the Swiss master cheesemaker Maurizio Lorenzetti, who helps the family produce the amazing Swiss-Italian-style cheeses Nicasio has become renowned for.

One day we saw the Nicasio booth at a farmers' market in Davis, California, and we asked the dairymen how they liked to cook their cheese. They encouraged us to melt their bucolic and slightly allium-flavored Nicasio Square—a tame-smelling washed-rind cheese reminiscent of a young Taleggio—with spinach and pasta. It's a wonderful combination that highlights the earthy, mushroomy flavors of the cheese.

We serve this in mini-cocottes, which are small ceramic dishes (like ramekins) that hold roughly 6 ounces. Not only are they a perfect serving size, but they also make for an impressive presentation.

1. Preheat the oven to 375°F. Butter five 8-ounce mini-cocottes or ramekins.

2. Cook the pasta in a large pot of salted boiling water until al dente. Drain through a colander and toss with spinach. Spoon pasta and spinach into mini-cocottes until they are all very full, as the mornay will cause the noodles to settle to the bottom. Place the mini-cocottes on a rimmed baking sheet.

3. To prepare the mornay sauce, heat the milk in a small saucepan over medium heat. As soon as the milk starts to steam and tiny bubbles form around the edges of the pan, turn off the heat. Place the butter in a medium saucepan and melt over medium flame. Add the flour and stir with a flat-edge wooden paddle just until the roux begins to take on a light brown color, scraping the bottom to prevent burning, about 3 minutes. Slowly add the milk and stir constantly until the sauce thickens enough to evenly coat the back of a spoon—a finger drawn along the back of the spoon should leave a clear swath. Stir in chili flakes, salt, and pepper, and cook for another minute. Remove from heat and add cheese to sauce, stirring until completely melted. Pour over the pasta and spinach in mini-cocottes.

4. Bake for 25 to 30 minutes, or until the contents of the mini-cocottes are bubbly and the cheese browns on top.

SMOKED IDIAZABAL
MASON-JAR POTPIES WITH LAMB AND TOMATO SAUCE

SERVES 4

¾ pound ground lamb, crumbled into small chunks

6 tablespoons butter, divided

½ cup plus 5 tablespoons flour, divided

⅛ teaspoon sugar

¼ teaspoon sea salt

10 ounces Idiazabal, rind removed, shredded, divided

1 tablespoon ice water

6 cups tomato juice

Sea salt

Freshly ground black pepper

8 ounces elbow macaroni

Special equipment:

Rolling pin

4 (12-ounce) mason jars

IDIAZABAL IS A SMOKED SHEEP'S-MILK CHEESE WITH A LUSCIOUS FLAVOR UNLIKE ANY dairy treat you've ever tasted. Originating in the fields of the Basque countryside, Idiazabal retains the rich, nutty notes that are signature to sheep's milk. Its unique flavor comes from the fact that it is smoked over a series of woods, such as beech, cherry, and hawthorn, which impart a gentle smokiness to this eight-month-aged cheese.

When creating this dish, we had to consider which ingredients would stand up to the robust personality of sheep's milk while still playing well with the smokiness that makes Idiazabal such a prize. After much tasting—oh, the torments we endure for our craft!—we settled on ground lamb coupled with velvety, flour-thickened tomato sauce and topped with a potpie crust. A winner out of the gate, this dish was absolutely swoon-worthy from bite one. It is what lasagna dreams of being when it grows up

1. Preheat oven to 375°F.

2. Heat a saucepan over medium heat and brown lamb for about 3 minutes, or just until it is uniformly brown. You do not want to cook it completely; a tiny bit of pinkness is fine. Pour off fat from lamb, reserving about 3 tablespoons. Set reserved lamb fat in the refrigerator and put ground lamb aside to cool.

3. Chop 2 tablespoons of the butter into small chunks and place in the freezer for 5 minutes, reserving the remaining butter for the tomato sauce. Prepare the pie dough by combining ½ cup flour, sugar, salt, and 2 tablespoons of the shredded cheese in a food processor. Pulse a few times to mix completely. Add the reserved lamb fat and pulse a few more times, then add the butter from the freezer, pulsing until you've got lumps that are each about half the size of a pea. Trickle in 1 tablespoon of ice water, pulsing until the dough comes together into a ball. You may need to add another teaspoon of ice water.

4. Using a rolling pin, roll the dough to ¼ inch thick between two pieces of parchment. Turn a mason jar upside down and use it to cut out 4 jar-sized pie crusts. Remove the excess dough and store for another use if you like (or eat it straight up, like we did). Cut three 1-inch-long slices in the middle of each crust and slide the parchment paper with the dough into the refrigerator. These cuts will vent the dough, allowing steam to escape and keeping the crust intact.

5. To prepare the sauce, heat the tomato juice in a pot over medium heat. As soon as the juice starts to simmer, turn off the heat. Place the remaining 4 tablespoons of butter in a medium saucepan and melt over medium-low heat. ⏵ recipe continues

Add the remaining 5 tablespoons of flour and stir with a wooden spoon for about 2 minutes, or just until the roux begins to take on a beige color and smell nutty. Add the hot tomato juice, increase the heat to medium, and stir until the sauce thickens. Lower heat to medium-low, add a few shakes each of salt and pepper, and stir well. Remove from heat. Add ⅓ cup of shredded cheese, stirring constantly until completely melted. Set sauce aside, stirring occasionally to keep a skin from forming.

6. Cook the pasta in a large pot of salted boiling water until al dente. Drain thoroughly through a colander and set aside.

7. Ladle a 1-inch layer of tomato sauce into the bottom of each of four 12-ounce mason jars, followed by 3 tablespoons of pasta. Next, layer into each jar 3 tablespoons of cooked lamb, 3 tablespoons of shredded cheese, and another 1-inch layer of tomato sauce. At this point, the jars should be about halfway full. Repeat the layering process again—3 tablespoons of pasta, 3 tablespoons of lamb, and 3 tablespoons of cheese, leaving about 1 inch of space at the top of the jars. Fill the jars the rest of the way with sauce.

8. Poke a butter knife down into the middle of each jar and gently jiggle the knife to allow some of the sauce to trickle down between the layers. The level of sauce at the top of the jar should decrease, signifying that it is draining down—keep jiggling the knife until no more will flow to the bottom of the jar. Top off each jar with a little more sauce, leaving ½ inch of space at the rim of the jars.

9. Set a folded towel on the counter to protect the glass, and tap the bottom of the jars a few times to help the contents settle. Remove the pie crusts from the refrigerator and push one into each jar, so that the dough sits snugly on the surface of the sauce.

10. Place the jars on a rimmed baking sheet and slide into the oven. Bake for 30 minutes, or until the pie crust is crisp and the contents of the jars are bubbling excitedly. Carefully remove the jars from the oven—they'll be incredibly hot and very full!—and allow them to sit 15 minutes before serving. If you want to store them for later, allow the jars to cool completely before replacing the lids of the mason jars and stashing them in the refrigerator for up to three days.

ALTERNATIVE CHEESES: Smokey Shepherd, Frere Fumant, Petit Basque

WINE PAIRINGS: Tempranillo, Garnacha, Côtes du Rhône reds, Barbera

ADDITIONAL PAIRINGS FOR THE CHEESE: Spanish date-and-almond cake, panforte, robust sausages, smoked Spanish paprika

STUFFED ZUCCHINI WITH SAN ANDREAS SHEEP'S-MILK CHEESE, CHERRY TOMATOES, AND MACARONI

SERVES 4 TO 6

3 pounds zucchini (about 2 large zucchini)

5 ounces elbow macaroni

1 cup milk

1 tablespoon butter

1 tablespoon flour

¼ teaspoon sea salt

¼ teaspoon freshly ground black pepper

¼ teaspoon chili flakes

7 ounces San Andreas cheese, shredded, divided

1 cup halved cherry tomatoes

Chili oil for topping

ALTERNATIVE CHEESES: aged Mahón, Matos Family's St. Jorge, Pecorino Foglie di Noce, Pecorino Ginepro

WINE PAIRINGS: dry rosés, Tocai Friulano, Grüner Veltliner, dry Rieslings

ADDITIONAL PAIRINGS FOR THE CHEESE: fava beans, ground black pepper, olive oil

WE'RE CONVINCED THAT OUR FRIEND AMBER STOTT, AN AVID AND TALENTED VEGETABLE gardener, is a masochist when it comes to zucchini. Every year she starts zucchini plants and nurtures them lovingly. In response, they grow to become brambled beasts that choke the neighboring plants and produce so many zucchini that they threaten to choke poor Amber too. She begs for recipes and pleads with friends to take some off her hands. How could we say no?

If you're under attack as well, this is a nifty way to take a few of those big green bad boys down. The zucchini are sliced lengthwise and hollowed out a bit before being stuffed with macaroni and cheese and fresh cherry tomatoes. (If you're gardening, you may very well have the tomatoes growing right next to your zucchini.) The entire thing is splashed with a bit of chili oil at the end for a slightly burned heat. We like to use a grassy, mild sheep's-milk cheese called San Andreas for this dish, as its green flavors pair well with the hot-weather produce.

We recommend you use two large zucchini for this dish, but a few smaller zucchini could work too. Each zucchini will stuff a bit differently based on its age and size, so use your best judgment.

1. Set up a large stockpot with 1 to 2 inches of water and a steamer basket. You should have enough water to steam but not so much that the zucchini sits in water. Bring to a boil over high heat. While the water heats, cut the zucchini in half lengthwise and, using a large spoon, scoop out the soft flesh and seeds and discard them. The outer flesh close to the skin should be firmer and resist scooping. Steam the hollowed zucchini for 8 to 10 minutes, or until soft. Place in a large, lightly greased baking dish and set aside.

2. Preheat oven to 350°F. Cook the pasta in a large pot of salted boiling water until al dente. Drain through a colander and set aside.

3. To prepare the mornay sauce, heat the milk in a small saucepan over medium heat. As soon as the milk starts to steam and tiny bubbles form around the edges of the pan, turn off the heat. Place the butter in a medium saucepan and melt over medium flame. Add the flour and stir with a flat-edge wooden paddle just until the roux begins to take on a light brown color, scraping the bottom to prevent burning, about 3 minutes. Slowly add the milk and stir constantly until the sauce thickens enough to evenly coat the back of a spoon—a finger drawn along the back of the spoon should leave a clear swath. Remove from heat and stir in salt, pepper, and chili flakes. Add 5 ounces of the cheese to sauce, stirring until completely melted. Season with more salt and pepper to taste.

4. Fold the sauce and cherry tomatoes into the pasta. Spoon macaroni and cheese into the hollowed-out zucchini and top with remaining cheese. Bake for 25 to 30 minutes. Serve in slices, drizzled with chili oil.

ROQUEFORT MACARONI
WITH BEETS, SHALLOTS, AND POPPY SEEDS

SERVES 4

1   **pound red beets, trimmed of their leaves**

2   **tablespoons olive oil**

10 **ounces elbow macaroni**

1   **tablespoon butter**

1   **tablespoon minced shallots**

1½ **cups heavy cream**

1   **ounce Parmesan, finely grated**

8   **ounces Roquefort, broken apart, divided**

    Pinch of sea salt

    Pinch of freshly ground black pepper

1   **tablespoon poppy seeds, plus extra for topping**

ALTERNATIVE CHEESES:
Most sweet, buttery, and mild sheep's-milk blues will play a worthwhile understudy to Roquefort, but we especially recommend Ewe's Blue by Old Chatham Sheepherding Co., Bohemian Blue by Hidden Springs Creamery, and Big Woods Blue by Shepherd's Way.

WINE PAIRINGS: dry Chenin Blanc, Tocai Friulano, Grüner Veltliner

ADDITIONAL PAIRINGS FOR THE CHEESE: quince jam, local honey with honeycomb, fresh pears

ROQUEFORT IS A CLASSIC BLUE, AND FOR A VERY GOOD REASON. MADE OF FATTY, buttery sheep's milk, Roquefort is creamier and saltier than either Stilton or Gorgonzola—mouthwateringly so—yet without that oh-so-fearsome "blue bite" that many fiery blues possess. These are the qualities that make the pairing of Roquefort with earthy-sweet beets so darn appealing.

Beets and poppy seeds are a lovely combination with roots in northeastern Italy. Thanks to the beets, this bright pink macaroni and cheese isn't just lovely to look at but also delightful to taste.

1. Preheat oven to 400°F. Line a rimmed baking sheet with aluminum foil. Spread beets onto foil, rub them with olive oil, and cover them with another sheet of foil. Roast for 1 to 2 hours, checking the beets every 15 minutes after the first hour. They're done when they can be easily pierced with a fork. When the beets are cool enough to handle, peel off the skins and puree the beets in a food processor until smooth.

2. Cook the pasta in a large pot of salted boiling water until al dente. Drain through a colander and set aside.

3. Place the butter in a saucepan over medium-high heat. When the butter is melted, add shallots and sauté until fragrant and soft, about 3 to 5 minutes. Add the cream and heat just until bubbles form around the edge of the pan and the cream begins to steam. Add the Parmesan, 4 ounces of the Roquefort, beet puree, salt, and pepper, and stir together. The dish will be very hot pink (think anything worn by Molly Ringwald in the '80s). Stir in the cooked pasta and poppy seeds.

4. Place in an 8-by-8-inch buttered baking dish and top with remaining Roquefort and a last sprinkle of additional poppy seeds if desired. Bake for 15 to 18 minutes, or until the edges are bubbly and the Roquefort has melted. Allow to cool for 5 minutes before serving.

Note: *The beet greens should not be wasted! They are very similar to Swiss chard and can be treated the same way. Chop them up and sauté them with a glug of olive oil and a dash of chili flakes, salt, and pepper. Once they're limp, add a splash of red wine or cider vinegar to make a perfect complementary side dish.*

TUNA NOODLE CASSEROLE

SERVES 4 TO 6

- **4** tablespoons butter, divided
- **1** small onion, finely chopped
- **8** ounces cremini mushrooms, sliced thickly
- **¼** cup dry sherry
- **1½** cups chicken broth
- **1½** cups whole milk
- **¼** cup flour
- **2** teaspoons lemon juice
- **¼** teaspoon sea salt
- **⅛** teaspoon freshly ground black pepper
- **⅓** cup fresh or frozen peas
- **6** ounces Barber's English Cheddar, shredded, divided
- **1** (5-ounce) can tuna in water, drained
- **6** ounces egg noodles
- **1** cup coarse breadcrumbs
- **1** ounce Parmesan, grated

ALTERNATIVE CHEESES: Kerrygold Cheddar, Black Diamond Cheddar, Petaluma Cheddar (really, any extra-sharp, semifirm Cheddar will do wonderfully)

WINE PAIRINGS: dry or off-dry Chenin Blanc, dry Riesling, Grenache Blanc, Ribolla Gialla, Pinot Noir

ADDITIONAL PAIRINGS FOR THE CHEESE: salami, fennel, heirloom apples

TUNA NOODLE CASSEROLE. ARE THERE ANY OTHER WORDS MORE RETRO OR NOSTALGIA-inducing? Many of us grew up on the casserole made with the stuff from the box, which, as much as we bash it, admittedly had its charms. However, the real dish—with spiky-sharp Cheddar cheese, mushrooms soaked in dry sherry, and garden-fresh peas—is a far cry from the five-minute-meal variety. Stick with canned albacore tuna for that old-school flavor that fresh fish just can't deliver.

This dish is an oft-overlooked macaroni-and-cheese classic: fast, affordable, and incredibly easy to make. Barber's 1833 English Reserve Cheddar is as sharp and dry as London wit and gives a nice bite to this dish. The real star may very well be the Cheddary breadcrumb crust, which you'll find perfectly salty and as crisp as a heat-tempered cracker.

1. Preheat oven to 375°F and butter a 2-quart baking dish. In a large skillet, melt 1 tablespoon of the butter over medium heat. Add the onions and cook for 3 minutes, stirring to keep them from burning, until they have softened a little. Add the mushrooms, turn the heat up to high, and sauté, stirring occasionally. Just as you think the mushrooms are about to burn, they'll suddenly give up their liquid and begin to squeak a bit. Once the water evaporates, add the sherry and continue to cook, stirring occasionally, until the liquid has evaporated. Remove from heat and set aside.

2. Heat the broth and milk in a small saucepan over medium heat. As soon as they start to steam and form tiny bubbles around the edges, turn off the heat. Place the remaining 3 tablespoons of butter in a medium saucepan and melt over medium flame. Add the flour and stir with a flat-edge wooden paddle just until the roux begins to take on a light brown color, scraping the bottom to prevent burning, about 3 minutes. Slowly add the hot milk and broth, stirring constantly until the sauce thickens enough to evenly coat the back of a spoon—a finger drawn along the back of the spoon should leave a clear swath. Simmer for another 3 minutes, stirring constantly. Add the lemon juice, salt, pepper, peas, and 2 ounces of the Cheddar. Gently fold in the tuna so that you still have some large chunks.

3. Cook the pasta in a large pot of salted boiling water until al dente. Drain through a colander. Toss the noodles, mushrooms, and onions with the sauce and pour into the greased baking dish.

4. In a bowl, toss together the breadcrumbs, Parmesan, and remaining Cheddar. Blanket the top of the casserole with the cheese and crumbs. Bake for 20 to 25 minutes, or until the edges are bubbling and the top has turned a golden brown. Cool for 5 minutes before serving.

BRILLAT-SAVARIN WITH FUSILLI,
PEARS, FENNEL, AND TORN CROISSANT TOPPING

SERVES 2 TO 4

4	tablespoons fennel seeds
8	ounces fusilli
3	tablespoons olive oil
1	medium bulb fennel, sliced paper thin
2	tablespoons water
2	cups milk
2	tablespoons butter
3	tablespoons flour
½	teaspoon sea salt
½	teaspoon freshly ground white pepper
1	pound Brillat-Savarin, rind carefully peeled off, chopped into large chunks
3	French butter pears, peeled and chopped into ½-inch cubes
1	large croissant, torn into small pieces by hand

ALTERNATIVE CHEESES:
Délice d'Argental, Délice de Bourgogne, Cowgirl Creamery's Mt. Tam, Sweet Grass's Green Hill

ALTERNATIVE FRUITS:
Bosc pears, Anjou pears, Seckel pears, Comice pears

WINE PAIRINGS:
Chardonnay, champagne, dry Riesling

ADDITIONAL PAIRINGS FOR THE CHEESE: toasted hazelnuts, spiced pear compote, cornmeal biscuits

WE'VE HEARD BRILLAT-SAVARIN CALLED "THE ICE CREAM OF CHEESE," AND IT IS INDEED something special. When ripe, this French triple-cream develops a lusciously rich, buttery texture that begs to be eaten straight up, perhaps with a tiny spoon.

Named after the eighteenth-century French gourmand, Brillat-Savarin is produced in the Normandy region of France, where the cows are known for their profoundly rich milk. When you buy this cheese, make sure it is soft and gives way under a gentle touch; if it doesn't, allow it to ripen in your refrigerator for up to a week to achieve its signature smooth, buttery body.

This dish is all about subtlety. It's not bursting with flavor like some of the other recipes in this book—rather, it's a soft, pure, textural treat. We recommend removing the rind before chopping, but peel carefully—you don't want to waste even a morsel of this lovely cheese, especially the perfectly ripe outer layers!

1. Heat a small saucepan over medium-high heat. Add fennel seeds and toast until they are fragrant and start to darken just a touch, agitating them constantly. Remove from heat.

2. Cook the pasta in salted boiling water until al dente. Drain through a colander and set aside.

3. In a large pan, heat olive oil over medium-high heat. Add sliced fennel bulb and cook for 5 minutes, stirring occasionally. Add water and continue cooking until soft but still toothsome, with a touch of caramelization, about 5 more minutes. Set aside.

4. To prepare the mornay sauce, heat the milk in a small saucepan over medium heat. As soon as the milk starts to steam and tiny bubbles form around the edges of the pan, turn off the heat. Place the butter in a medium saucepan and melt over medium flame. Add the flour and stir with a flat-edge wooden paddle just until the roux begins to take on a light brown color, scraping the bottom to prevent burning, about 3 minutes. Slowly add the milk and stir constantly until the sauce thickens enough to evenly coat the back of a spoon—a finger drawn along the back of the spoon should leave a clear swath. Remove from heat and stir in salt and pepper. Add cheese to sauce, stirring until completely melted.

5. Preheat your broiler. In a shallow casserole dish, combine pasta, cheese sauce, sautéed fennel bulb, and pears. Fold gently until well combined. Cover the top of the dish with torn croissant chunks and slide under the broiler. Broil just until the top of the cheese is bubbling and the croissant bits are toasty. Dish into bowls and sprinkle lightly with toasted fennel seeds.

PENNE WITH GARROTXA,
SERRANO HAM, AND SUN-DRIED TOMATOES

SERVES 2 TO 4

8 ounces penne

1 pound Garrotxa, shredded

¼ cup milk

½ cup crème fraîche

1 tablespoon butter

½ teaspoon freshly ground white pepper

⅓ cup chopped sun-dried tomatoes

6 ounces Serrano ham slices, torn coarsely by hand into chunks

NATIVE TO CATALONIA, SPAIN, GARROTXA IS A THROATY, GOATY CHEESE THAT IMPARTS an almost Cheddar-like tanginess. A gray mold blankets this pasteurized flavor titan, which gets its smooth earthiness from the lush coastal grasses that feed the goats raised to make it. Cutting away the rind on this firm cheese is easy, and a sharp knife run down the sides will shave off the moldy exterior without sacrificing much of the Garrotxa beneath.

Here, Garrotxa coalesces with two other signature Spanish ingredients, sun-dried tomatoes and Serrano ham, to create an ethereal cheese gratin polished with just a touch of butter, milk, and crème fraîche. This recipe isn't your typical melty, creamy macaroni and cheese; rather, it's a drier dish that allows the ingredients to mingle coyly while remaining somewhat independent.

1. Preheat oven to 375°F.

2. Cook the pasta in salted boiling water until al dente. Drain through a colander. Set aside.

3. In a saucepan, combine cheese, milk, crème fraîche, and butter. Cook over medium-low heat until cheese is mostly melted and you have a creamy sauce. To keep the cheese sauce from breaking, remove the sauce from the heat before the cheese is entirely melted. Season with pepper, adding more to taste if you like.

4. In a shallow buttered casserole dish, toss pasta with sun-dried tomatoes and Serrano ham. Pour the sauce over the pasta, then stir together until combined. Bake for 15 to 20 minutes, until the top is golden brown and bubbling around the edges. Serve immediately.

ALTERNATIVE CHEESES: Ibores, Twig Farm Goat Tomme, Bardwell Farm's Equinox

WINE PAIRINGS: Txakoli, Catalonian white wine, Grüner Veltliner

ADDITIONAL PAIRINGS FOR THE CHEESE: fig jam, picholine olives

PASTA FRITTATA WITH
TALEGGIO, MUSHROOMS, AND TRUFFLE OIL

SERVES 2 AS AN ENTRÉE,
4 AS A SIDE

- **5** ounces elbow macaroni
- **6** large eggs
- **1** tablespoon milk
- **½** teaspoon sea salt
- **¼** teaspoon freshly ground black pepper
- **1** small portobello mushroom, stem removed, cut in half and thinly sliced
- **6** ounces Taleggio, rind removed, chopped into ½-inch cubes
- **2** ounces salami, cut into thin strips
- **1** teaspoon black or white truffle oil, or more to taste

AH, TALEGGIO . . . AN ITALIAN FERMENTED-MILK CLASSIC. SOME DESCRIBE TALEGGIO'S funky perfume as a stench that causes flowers to wilt and nearby children to burst into tears. This is all due to the fact that it's a washed-rind cheese, meaning the outer part of the cheese is patted down with a salted brine as it ages.

Don't let the ripe smell drive you away. Embrace the funk. The taste is beefy, lactic, and much sweeter than the smell suggests. Indeed, there's a reason Taleggio is considered one of the best washed-rind cheeses in the world.

This macaroni-and-cheese dish comes in the form of a frittata, with the egg and cheese binding together aged salami and dry-sautéed mushrooms. While delicious for dinner, this recipe is equally appropriate for a sophisticated brunch with friends. If you can find farm-fresh eggs, their heartier flavor will greatly accentuate the delights of the cheese.

1. Cook the pasta in a large pot of salted boiling water until al dente. Drain through a colander and set aside.

2. Whisk together the eggs and milk. Season with salt and pepper and set aside. Preheat the oven to 375°F.

3. Place a sauté pan over high heat. Once hot, add the mushrooms and reduce heat to medium. (This is a dry sauté: a sauté without oil.) The mushrooms will slowly release their liquids and cook through. Keep stirring and tossing. The mushrooms may squeak a bit as they cook, and you may feel they're about to burn. Don't worry: they will soon reabsorb their water and shrink in size. Once the mushrooms are softened, toss with a pinch of salt and remove from heat. Set aside.

4. Lightly grease an 8-by-8-inch baking dish with butter. Toss the pasta, Taleggio, salami, and mushrooms together in the baking dish. Pour the eggs and milk over the top. Make sure all pasta is covered by egg, pushing any errant noodles under with your fingers. Bake for 35 to 40 minutes, or until lightly browned on top. Allow to cool for 5 minutes. Drizzle the top lightly with truffle oil and serve immediately.

ALTERNATIVE CHEESES: Nicasio Square, Meadow Creek Grayson, Quadrello di Bufala, Twin Maple Farms Hudson Red

WINE PAIRINGS: Chardonnay, Nebbiolo, Pinot Noir

ADDITIONAL PAIRINGS FOR THE CHEESE: honey, pickled onions

THE SWEET WORLD OF STINKY CHEESES—
THE SOURCE OF THE SMELL

A GOOD WASHED-RIND CHEESE CAN LET OFF a pungent, footy funk strong enough to peel paint off the wall. The reason? Washed-rind cheeses have been bathed in a saline solution, and this washing helps the cheese retain moisture and develop its signature flavors. The resulting cheese usually possesses a lovely interior that makes enduring the smell worthwhile.

But what exactly causes this infamous, um, aroma? Due to the washing process, the outside of the cheese develops a cultivation of *Brevibacterium linens*, otherwise known as *B. linens.* These bacteria cultures, which grow in hues ranging from bright pink to dusty adobe, are what cause the strong smell. Fun (if slightly off-putting) fact: These very same cultures are responsible for foot odor.

A cheese's bathing solution doesn't have to be entirely about the salt. Many varieties, such as Appenzeller, are washed in solutions flecked with locally grown herbs. Some, such as Pedrozo Dairy's Bubbly Cow, are moistened with a boozy bath of sparkling wine. Cheeses can be bathed in anything from spirits to apple cider, and each ingredient lends something to the cheese's color, aroma, and flavor.

Some washed rinds are stinkier than others; Époisses, a patently silky cheese, carries with it quite an odiferous funk despite its earthy, grassy inner layers. Taleggio, in the middle ground of stinkiness, also hides within its depths a sweet, meaty treat that contrasts with its rind's aroma. Other washed rinds, like Gruyère and Comté, don't smell that strongly at all. Are you sensing a pattern here? A cheese's smell tells little about the flavor wrapped safely inside the rind.

When buying a washed-rind cheese, look for rinds that are uniformly pink, orange, or light beige. A bit of mottling is fine, but if you see too much splotchiness, be wary. Any large, spooky mold growing vertically off the cheese is an indicator that something has gone terribly wrong.

The smell of a washed-rind cheese may be strong and pungent, sometimes akin to a teenager's beloved and abused sneaker. If your cheese possesses a particularly strong ammoniated funk, this may mean the cheese has spoiled. (Don't worry: You'll be able to tell.) With a few exceptions, the skin should be smooth and perhaps a little bit slippery, but be cautious of anything slimy. A washed-rind cheese that is dry or cracked is tragically dehydrated and has gone to the great cheese shop in the sky.

When in doubt, though, ask your cheesemonger. Sometimes a washed-rind cheese may seem zombified to a beginner when in reality it is at its peak ripeness. If your cheesemonger gives you the go-ahead, give it a try! Don't let a pungent aroma deter you from trying an unfamiliar washed-rind cheese. You may be surprised at how dreamy the cheese itself tastes.

Washed-rind cheeses worth trying:

- STINKING BISHOP
- ÉPOISSES
- LIMBURGER
- MUENSTER
- TALEGGIO
- APPENZELLER
- AFFIDELICE
- NICASIO SQUARE
- RACLETTE
- PEDROZO DAIRY'S BUBBLY COW
- RED HAWK
- STOUT COW
- VACHERIN MONT D'OR
- CATO CORNER'S HOOLIGAN
- TWIN MAPLE HUDSON RED
- ROBIOLA LOMBARDIA

PEPPERS STUFFED WITH
MITICREMA AND TOASTED ORZO

SERVES 4 TO 6

- 6   medium bell peppers, either red, orange, or yellow, of uniform size
- 4   ounces Kalamata olives, pitted and chopped
- 2   medium heirloom tomatoes, chopped fine (don't peel them or remove the seeds)
- 8   ounces Miticrema, crumbled
- 2   teaspoons lemon juice, from 1 medium lemon
- ¼   teaspoon sea salt
- ¼   teaspoon freshly ground black pepper
- 4   ounces pine nuts
- 7   ounces orzo
- 1   tablespoon olive oil
- ½   small red onion, chopped fine
- 6   round slices of lemon

NOT MANY PEOPLE HAVE HEARD OF MITICREMA, A SOFT, FRESH SHEEP'S-MILK CHEESE from the Murcia region of Spain. Its fluffy consistency often leads people to believe it will be a sweet cheese, but one taste reveals Miticrema as a tangy, salty experience with a touch of acidity. It's like the girl in high school who is all sweetness and sunshine from a distance but turns out to be a sassy tart once you get to know her.

This dish is inspired by a stuffed-pepper recipe that I developed many, many (many...) years ago, when I first learned to cook. I discovered early on that fresh cheese and Kalamata olives are a sure bet for flavor, and the addition of ripe heirloom tomatoes and sautéed red onions guarantees happy dinner guests. I've also added toasted orzo, which has a rich nuttiness that makes these stuffed peppers the perfect vegetarian comfort food. This dish is certainly not your average gooey macaroni and cheese, but we hope it will expand your thinking when it comes to what makes a mac, well, a mac.

If you like, you can prepare the stuffing a night ahead. Try to resist eating it all with a spoon—it's just that good.   —SS

1.   Preheat oven to 350°F.

2.   Using a sharp knife, carefully cut around the stem of each pepper and remove it, leaving the pepper with an opening big enough for it to be stuffed. Clean out any seeds and white, sinewy bits. Set the peppers aside in a baking dish large enough to accommodate them all, opening side up.

3.   In a large bowl, combine chopped olives, tomatoes, crumbled Miticrema, lemon juice, sea salt, and black pepper. Stir to combine and set aside.

4.   In a frying pan over medium heat, toast the nuts until they darken slightly and become fragrant, shaking the pan every minute or so to keep them from burning. Remove from heat. Once they are cool, coarsely chop the pine nuts and add them to the large bowl with the olives and cheese. Set aside.

5.   In the same pan, toast the dry pasta over medium heat, tossing gently every few minutes to keep it from burning. The pasta is done when the noodles develop a nutty fragrance and turn a darker shade of beige—some finer brands will turn a lovely rose color as they toast. Set pasta aside to cool, and set a pot of salted water to boil.

6.   In the same pan, heat olive oil over medium flame. Cook onions until they are brown and smell sweet, about 10 minutes, stirring every few minutes to keep them from burning. If you need to, sprinkle them with a touch of water to prevent them from singeing. Add onions to the large bowl with the olives and cheese, stirring to combine before setting aside. ❱❱ recipe continues

7. Cook the toasted pasta in the pot of salted boiling water for about 4 minutes; the orzo should be firm and toothsome, especially in the middle. Drain through a colander and add to the bowl with everything else, stirring well.

8. Use a spoon to stuff the peppers with filling, making sure there are no empty spaces. Gently tap the peppers on a hard surface to settle the filling, and then top them off with a little more. Set the stuffed peppers back in the baking dish and top each pepper with a slice of lemon. Slide the baking dish into the oven and cook for 55 minutes. Allow to sit for 5 minutes before serving.

A note on selecting bell peppers: *Try to pick peppers that can stand up on their bottoms without tipping. Peppers with uneven bases will make for a harrowing (and messy) baking experience. If all else fails, you can stick any tipsy peppers in a ramekin and set them in the baking dish to keep them upright.*

ALTERNATIVE CHEESES: any high-quality feta, Caña de Oveja, Nuvola di Pecora

WINE PAIRINGS: Verdelho, Torrontés, Godello

ADDITIONAL PAIRINGS FOR THE CHEESE: *membrillo* (quince jam), fig jam, black pepper, radicchio, roasted beets

THREE-CHEESE MACARONI CASSEROLE
WITH BROCCOLI, PANCETTA, AND SWEET PUGLIESE TOPPING

SERVES 4

- 12 ounces elbow macaroni
- ½ pound thick-cut pancetta, chopped coarsely (about 1 cup)
- 2½ cups milk
- 2 tablespoons butter
- 2 tablespoons flour
- 1 teaspoon sea salt
- ½ teaspoon freshly ground black pepper
- 6 ounces Pineland six-month-aged Cheddar, grated
- 4 ounces Monterey Jack, grated
- 4 ounces low-moisture (dry) mozzarella, chopped coarsely
- 1½ cups 1-inch chopped broccoli florets
- 2 cups coarsely torn sweet Pugliese bread, or other crusty non-sourdough variety
- ¼ cup chopped fresh chives

ALTERNATIVE CHEESES: Any medium-sharp Cheddar will work. Try Keen's Cheddar, Milton's Prairie Breeze, or Beehive's Promontory. Feel free to use any Jack or dry mozzarella.

WINE PAIRINGS: Gamay, Primitivo, Syrah

ADDITIONAL PAIRINGS FOR THE CHEESE: citrus marmalade, Spanish chorizo

WHEN YOU THINK OF THE STATE OF MAINE, DO YOU THINK OF CHEESE? NEITHER DID WE. Imagine our surprise when we tasted Pineland's six-month-aged Cheddar, a rich, regal cheese minus the diva personality. Creamy and smooth in texture, this easygoing Cheddar feels like it was produced with macaroni and cheese in mind.

This recipe mixes Pineland with your standard Monterey Jack, which provides a beguilingly smooth mouthfeel, and with dry mozzarella, which brings a joyful stringiness to the game. Pancetta lends a few enticing salty notes, while broccoli shakes up the texture and adds a little greenery to the landscape. If you prefer a drier, less velvety macaroni and cheese, decrease the amount of milk to 2 cups. The casserole will still be a flavor revelation, though the texture will be firmer and more fork-friendly.

1. Preheat oven to 350°F.

2. Cook the pasta in a large pot of salted boiling water until al dente. Drain through a colander and set aside.

3. Set a frying pan over medium heat and cook pancetta until it is good and crispy, about 5 minutes, stirring occasionally. Remove from heat, reserving both the pancetta and its fat.

4. To prepare the mornay sauce, heat the milk in a small saucepan over medium heat. As soon as the milk starts to steam and tiny bubbles form around the edges of the pan, turn off the heat. Place the butter in a medium saucepan and melt over medium flame. Add the flour and stir with a flat-edge wooden paddle just until the roux begins to take on a light brown color, scraping the bottom to prevent burning, about 3 minutes. Slowly add the milk and stir constantly until the sauce thickens enough to evenly coat the back of a spoon—a finger drawn along the back of the spoon should leave a clear swath. Remove from heat and stir in salt and pepper. Add all cheeses to sauce, stirring until completely melted.

5. In a 9-by-13-inch buttered baking pan, toss together pasta, broccoli, and pancetta with its fat, combining well. Cover with mornay sauce and gently fold into pasta. Spread with torn sweet Pugliese bread and bake for 30 minutes, or until the bread browns and the cheese is bubbling joyfully. Remove from oven and allow to sit for 10 minutes. Serve sprinkled generously with chopped fresh chives.

MEADOWKAAS AND
CHICKEN SAUSAGE SKILLET

SERVES 4

- **3** tablespoons sunflower oil or other high-smoke-point cooking oil
- **½** medium onion, chopped
- **½** pound chicken sausage, removed from casings and crumbled
- **1** red bell pepper, seeded and chopped
- **⅓** pound baby arugula leaves
- **10** ounces conchiglie
- **1½** cups whole milk
- **1½** tablespoons butter
- **1½** tablespoons flour
- **¼** teaspoon sea salt
- **¼** teaspoon freshly ground black pepper
- **2** teaspoons lemon zest
- **8** ounces Meadowkaas, rind removed, shredded
- **4** ounces Gruyère, rind removed, shredded

Chopped arugula leaves, for garnish

Lemon wedges, for garnish

ALTERNATIVE CHEESES: Two Sisters Isabella, Honey Bzzz, Petit Basque

WINE PAIRINGS: Grüner Veltliner, dry Riesling, darker-hued rosé, Barbera, Nero d'Avola

ADDITIONAL PAIRINGS FOR THE CHEESE: pumpernickel or rye bread, whole-grain mustard, apricots

MEADOWKAAS, AN INCREDIBLY RICH, SMOOTH DUTCH CHEESE, WAS MADE FOR MACARONI. This creamy variety is produced during the spring, when the cattle of Rouveen, Holland, graze only on fresh meadow grass and thus yield only fresh, meadowy milk. (Hence the name, which translates to "meadow cheese.") Meadowkaas is then aged for four weeks, which allows the springtime flavor and fatty texture to fully bloom.

When mixed with Gruyère and poured over a bittersweet combination of arugula and red bell peppers, Meadowkaas leads a parade of color, flavor, and texture. Chicken sausage brings a meaty layer to the dish without adding a ton of extra fat. This pan-to-oven casserole is made in a heavy skillet, though you could just as easily make it in a saucepan on the stovetop and pour it into a large casserole dish or Dutch oven to bake it.

1. Preheat oven to 350°F. Add sunflower oil to a heavy skillet with an ovenproof handle and set over medium heat. Once the oil shimmers, add the onions and cook until they begin to brown, stirring occasionally to keep them from burning. Add crumbled chicken sausage and cook until the meat is slightly browned, about 5 minutes. Add peppers and cook for 2 minutes, then add the arugula and cook for another 2 minutes. Remove from heat and set aside.

2. Cook the pasta in a large pot of salted boiling water until al dente. Drain through a colander and toss with the sausage mixture.

3. To prepare the mornay sauce, heat the milk in a small saucepan over medium heat. As soon as the milk starts to steam and tiny bubbles form around the edges of the pan, turn off the heat. Place the butter in a medium saucepan and melt over medium flame. Add the flour and stir with a flat-edge wooden paddle just until the roux begins to take on a light brown color, scraping the bottom to prevent burning, about 3 minutes. Slowly add the milk and stir constantly until the sauce thickens enough to evenly coat the back of a spoon—a finger drawn along the back of the spoon should leave a clear swath. Lower heat to medium-low, add salt, pepper, and lemon zest, and cook for another minute. Remove from heat and add both cheeses to the sauce, stirring until completely melted.

4. Once the cheese has melted into the sauce, pour the sauce over the pasta and sausage. Slide the skillet into the oven and cook for 30 minutes. Serve hot, sprinkled with chopped arugula leaves and accompanied by lemon wedges.

GRUYÈRE AND EMMENTALER
MACARONI WITH HAM AND CUBED SOURDOUGH

SERVES 4

- 10 ounces elbow macaroni
- 2 cups whole milk
- 2 tablespoons butter
- 2 tablespoons flour
- ½ teaspoon sea salt
- ¼ teaspoon freshly ground black pepper
- 2 tablespoons Dijon mustard
- 10 ounces Gruyère, shredded
- 8 ounces Emmentaler, shredded
- 8 ounces Black Forest ham, cut into ½-inch cubes
- 2 cups sourdough bread cubes, each about ½ inch square, crust on

GRUYÈRE, NAMED AFTER THE SWISS DISTRICT OF GRUYÈRE, IS A LOVELY, HARD COW'S-milk cheese known the world over for its seductively melty personality. Luscious and smooth, Gruyère is often paired with Emmentaler to make what can only be described as a superlative fondue.

With Gruyère and Emmentaler intertwined in a heady embrace, we toss Black Forest ham into the mix, making for a sultry ménage à trois of flavor and texture. Topped with chunky cubed sourdough for crunch, this dish is more than delicious—it's sinful.

1. Preheat the oven to 350°F. Lightly butter an 8-by-8-inch baking dish.

2. Cook the pasta in a large pot of salted boiling water until al dente. Drain through a colander and set aside.

3. To prepare the mornay sauce, heat the milk in a small saucepan over medium heat. As soon as the milk starts to steam and tiny bubbles form around the edges of the pan, turn off the heat. Place the butter in a medium saucepan and melt over medium flame. Add the flour and stir with a flat-edge wooden paddle just until the roux begins to take on a light brown color, scraping the bottom to prevent burning, about 3 minutes. Slowly add the milk and stir constantly until the sauce thickens enough to evenly coat the back of a spoon—a finger drawn along the back of the spoon should leave a clear swath. Remove from heat and stir in salt and pepper. Add mustard and cheese to sauce, stirring until completely melted.

4. Pour pasta into greased baking dish and toss with ham. Pour the cheese sauce over the top of the pasta and stir gently to incorporate into the ham and noodles. Top liberally with bread cubes, slide into the oven, and bake for 30 minutes. Let sit 10 minutes before serving.

ALTERNATIVE CHEESES: Any reputable Gruyère and Emmentaler will go well in this recipe. Ask your local cheesemonger.

WINE PAIRINGS: Viognier, Altesse, Roussanne, Pinot Noir, dry rosé

ADDITIONAL PAIRINGS FOR THE CHEESE: toasted walnuts, bacon, crusty bread

TURKEY AND ROBUSTO
MAC-AND-CHEESELETS

MAKES 12 TO 16 MAC-
AND-CHEESELETS

8   ounces elbow macaroni

6   ounces cooked turkey, shredded (about 1¼ cups)

12 ounces Robusto, shredded, divided

3   tablespoons chopped fresh sage

2   eggs

2   cups milk

2   tablespoons olive oil

2   tablespoons flour

½   teaspoon sea salt

    Freshly ground black pepper

1   cup leftover cranberry sauce or cranberry jam (see recipe on page 156)

ONE OF THE BEST THINGS ABOUT COOKING A BIG OL' THANKSGIVING TURKEY IS THE leftovers. The carcass goes to making turkey stock, the legs are best saved for eating while watching television, and the last little bits of meat are reserved for all manner of dishes, from posole to sandwiches.

Or, perhaps, turkey macaroni and cheese.

Cooked in a muffin tin, these adorable individual mac-and-cheeselets are a good way to exercise portion control (assuming you eat just one or two and not, like, seven). Robusto is a Gouda-style cheese made with the cultures used for Parmesan, so it has a Gouda-like personality while maintaining the sharp nuttiness that makes Parmesan so delightful.

The recipe for cranberry jam on page 156 is a festive addition to this dish, adding grace to the turkey and cheese. If you're making the mac-and-cheeselets after Thanksgiving and have leftover cranberry sauce, feel free to use that instead.

1. Cook the pasta in a large pot of salted boiling water until al dente. Drain through a colander and rinse with cool water to stop the cooking process. Drain again and set aside.

2. Once the macaroni has cooled, toss it with the turkey, 5 ounces of Robusto, and sage in a bowl and set aside. In another bowl, whisk the eggs and set aside.

3. Preheat oven to 375°F. To prepare the mornay sauce, heat the milk in a small saucepan over medium heat. As soon as the milk starts to steam and tiny bubbles form around the edges of the pan, turn off the heat. Place the olive oil in a medium saucepan and heat over medium flame. Add the flour and stir with a flat-edge wooden paddle just until the roux begins to take on a light brown color, scraping the bottom to prevent burning, about 3 minutes. Slowly add the milk and stir constantly until the sauce thickens enough to evenly coat the back of a spoon—a finger drawn along the back of the spoon should leave a clear swath. Remove from heat and stir in salt and pepper. Add 5 ounces of the remaining Robusto to sauce, reserving 2 ounces, and stir until completely melted.

4. Temper the eggs by slowly pouring ¼ cup of the mornay sauce into the bowl with the eggs while whisking continually. Once combined, add the eggs to the rest of the mornay and whisk together. Carefully fold the pasta into the mornay sauce.

5. Spoon macaroni and cheese into the cups of a well-greased muffin tin. Two or three good spoonfuls per cheeselet should be fine, and they shouldn't be too heaping big. Level with the pan is just enough. Top each with some of the remaining Robusto and bake for 20 to 25 minutes, or until the tops are slightly golden brown. Cool for 3 minutes and serve with a few spoonfuls of cranberry jam. » recipe continues

CRANBERRY JAM

½ cup water

1 cup sugar

½ cup orange juice

12 ounces whole fresh cranberries (if using frozen, defrost first)

1 teaspoon vanilla extract

¼ teaspoon butter

Place the water, sugar, and orange juice in a pot and bring to a boil. Add the cranberries, vanilla extract, and butter. Cook for about 10 to 15 minutes, or until the sauce has thickened up a bit. Serve hot, warm, or cold.

ALTERNATIVE CHEESES: Marieke Gouda, Willamette Valley Aged Gouda, Branched Oak Nettle Gouda, any excellent Dutch goat's-milk Gouda, Emmentaler, Gruyère

WINE PAIRINGS: Viognier, Rhône Valley white blends, rosé, Gamay, Pinot Noir

ADDITIONAL PAIRINGS FOR THE CHEESE: fenugreek, smoked country ham

BUFFALO CHICKEN MACARONI
WITH BUTTERMILK
BLUE CHEESE SAUCE

SERVES 8

2 boneless skinless chicken breasts

For the marinade:

1½ cups buttermilk

1 cup Buffalo wing sauce (such as Frank's)

For the macaroni and cheese:

10 ounces medium shell pasta

3 tablespoons olive oil, divided

2 stalks of celery, chopped

½ medium onion, chopped

1 clove garlic, minced

3 cups milk

¼ cup heavy cream

3 tablespoons butter

3 tablespoons flour

1 cup Buffalo wing sauce (such as Frank's)

Pinch of sea salt

Pinch of freshly ground black pepper

8 ounces aged firm Cheddar (such as Kerrygold), shredded

8 ounces Roth Käse Buttermilk Blue cheese, crumbled

8 ounces low-moisture (dry) mozzarella, shredded

⅓ cup chopped parsley

1 cup panko breadcrumbs

STEPHANIE AND I ALMOST CAME TO BLOWS OVER THIS RECIPE. SHE THOUGHT IT WOULD be a great jumping-off point, a twist on a familiar dish people could connect to. "Plus," she insisted, "it would taste outrageously good." I thought the idea had all the charm of a dilapidated Hooters bar. Lots of back-and-forth ensued, and finally Stephanie convinced me that we should give it a go.

Honestly, I hate it when she's right.

The recipe takes some patience and planning, but it is well worth the effort, as the result is mind-blowing. Chicken marinated overnight in buttermilk and Buffalo sauce is tossed with celery and pasta in a zesty mornay. The entire thing is covered with a smooth, tangy blue cheese sauce. (The sauce is also great on salads, by the way. I promise you'll never buy the premade stuff again.) The resulting mac is saucy, spicy, and scrumptious.

We love to use Roth Käse's Buttermilk Blue for this dish. It's a high-butterfat Wisconsin cheese with plenty of veining, a creamy blue with a gentle edge. —GM

1. Place the chicken breasts in a shallow pan or bowl with the buttermilk and 1 cup of Buffalo sauce. Cover with plastic wrap and allow to marinate in the refrigerator overnight.

2. Grease a 9-by-13-inch baking dish and preheat the oven to 375°F. Cook the pasta in a large pot of salted boiling water until al dente. Drain through a colander and set aside.

3. Chop the chicken breasts into bite-size pieces (which will be easy, as the chicken is now super-tender) and discard the marinade. In a saucepan, heat 1 tablespoon of olive oil over high heat. Working in batches, add the chicken and sear it on all sides. If you want a bit more kick, feel free to add a dash of Buffalo sauce to the chicken toward the end of the sear. Toss the chicken and the cooked pasta in the greased baking dish and set aside.

4. Add 1 tablespoon of olive oil to a saucepan over high heat. Toss in the celery and onion and cook for 2 minutes. Add garlic (and yet another dash of Buffalo sauce for more spice, if desired) and sauté for 30 more seconds. Remove vegetables from heat and add to the baking dish with chicken and pasta.

5. Prepare the mornay sauce. Heat the milk and cream in a small saucepan over medium heat. As soon as the mixture starts to steam and tiny bubbles form around the edges of the pan, turn off the heat. Place the butter in a medium saucepan and melt over medium heat. Add the flour and stir with a flat-edge wooden paddle just until the roux begins to take on a light brown color, scraping the bottom to prevent burning, about 3 minutes. recipe continues

For the blue cheese sauce:

- **6 ounces Roth Käse Buttermilk Blue**
- **½ cup buttermilk**
- **⅓ cup sour cream or yogurt**
- **¼ teaspoon Dijon mustard**
- **Pinch of salt**
- **Pinch of freshly ground black pepper**
- **1 tablespoon white vinegar**
- **1 tablespoon lemon juice**
- **1 tablespoon chopped chives**
- **1 tablespoon chopped parsley**

Slowly add the milk and cream mixture and stir constantly until the sauce thickens enough to evenly coat the back of a spoon—a finger drawn along the back of the spoon should leave a clear swath. Remove from heat. Add 1 cup of Buffalo sauce, salt, pepper, Cheddar cheese, and Buttermilk Blue and stir until smooth. Set aside.

6. Add the mozzarella to the baking dish and toss together with the other ingredients so it is evenly distributed. Pour the mornay sauce over the contents of the baking dish. In a small bowl, toss together the remaining 1 tablespoon of olive oil, parsley, and panko breadcrumbs, then distribute over the top of the baking dish. Bake for 35 to 40 minutes, or until thick and bubbly.

7. While the dish bakes in the oven, make the blue cheese sauce. Place Buttermilk Blue, buttermilk, sour cream or yogurt, mustard, salt, pepper, vinegar, and lemon juice in a blender and pulse a few times. Stir in the chives and parsley. Set aside until the pasta is done baking.

8. Allow casserole to cool for 5 minutes before serving. Serve topped with blue cheese sauce.

ALTERNATIVE CHEESES:
For blue: Gorgonzola, Shropshire, Stilton, Oregonzola, Point Reyes Blue
For Cheddar: Any aged, firm Cheddar will do.

WINE PAIRINGS: slightly sweet Riesling like a German Kabinett, an off-dry from Washington or New York state, Chenin Blanc from Vouvray

ADDITIONAL PAIRINGS FOR THE BUTTERMILK BLUE CHEESE: raspberry preserves, tea preserves, bacon, tomato

ALL KINDS OF CRISPY CRUSTS

IF YOU'VE EVER PREPARED A MACARONI-and-cheese casserole, you've likely sprinkled the top with breadcrumbs before sliding it into the oven, which allows the top to bake into a crispy brown crust. This is a lovely—and classic—way to top your baked mac and cheese, and our recipe for making breadcrumbs (page 22) is quick and foolproof. But there is a much larger world of textured toppings out there that is worth exploring. Below are just a few options to get you started; they can be used ground or whole, depending on your preferences. Don't be afraid to get creative!

- POPCORN
- PRETZELS
- ROASTED PUMPKIN SEEDS
- FLAX SEEDS
- BAGEL PIECES (PLAIN AND FLAVORED)
- SOAKED SUNFLOWER SEEDS
- WATER CRACKERS
- TRISCUITS
- TORTILLA CHIPS
- WHEAT CRISPS
- NONSUGARY CEREAL
- PITA BREAD
- TOASTED, COARSELY CHOPPED NUTS

You might also consider using interesting bread varieties to spice up your breadcrumb options:

- RYE BREAD
- SOURDOUGH
- PANKO
- SQUAW BREAD
- BRIOCHE
- CHALLAH
- FOCACCIA
- HAWAIIAN BREAD
- PUMPERNICKEL

CAHILL'S IRISH PORTER CHEDDAR
WITH BACON AND STOUT

SERVES 4 TO 6

10 ounces elbow macaroni

5 strips of thick-cut bacon, chopped (use the good stuff)

1 cup stout (plus the rest, you know, for you)

1½ cups milk

2 tablespoons butter

2 tablespoons flour

½ teaspoon sea salt

½ teaspoon freshly ground black pepper

12 ounces Cahill's Irish Porter Cheddar, shredded

¾ cup breadcrumbs

ALTERNATIVE CHEESES: Barely Buzzed, Keswick Creamery's Tommenator or Mad Tomme, Stout Cow, Kerrygold Dubliner with Irish Stout, Keen's Farmhouse Cheddar

WINE PAIRINGS: Zinfandel, a stout beer such as Guinness or Boddingtons

ADDITIONAL PAIRINGS FOR THE CHEESE: toasted walnuts, toasted hazelnuts, dark chocolate

AT FIRST GLANCE, CAHILL'S IRISH PORTER CHEDDAR LOOKS LIKE A LUSCIOUS SLICE OF marbled chocolate cake, or perhaps a wedge of fatty Italian charcuterie. Bite into it, though, and you'll discover something entirely different. This Irish Cheddar, created by Dave and Marion Cahill, is imbued with the unmistakably sharp, wheaty flavor of Irish stout. Guinness lovers will take note immediately, and any fan of high-personality cheese will appreciate this charismatic, though slightly tipsy, specimen.

1. Preheat oven to 375°F. Lightly butter the bottom and sides of a shallow casserole dish.

2. Cook the pasta in salted boiling water until almost al dente. Drain through a colander and set aside.

3. Add the bacon to a saucepan over medium heat. Cook until the bacon crisps up and releases its fat. Remove from heat and drain the excess fat by placing the bacon on a plate lined with paper towels. Clean the saucepan, pour in the stout, and bring to a boil over high heat. Reduce to medium and simmer until the stout is reduced by half.

4. To prepare the mornay sauce, heat the milk in a small saucepan over medium heat. As soon as the milk starts to steam and tiny bubbles form around the edges of the pan, turn off the heat. Place the butter in a medium saucepan and melt over medium flame. Add the flour and stir with a flat-edge wooden paddle just until the roux begins to take on a light brown color, scraping the bottom to prevent burning, about 3 minutes. Slowly add the milk and stir constantly until the sauce thickens enough to evenly coat the back of a spoon—a finger drawn along the back of the spoon should leave a clear swath. Slowly pour in stout, stir until well mixed, and cook until again thick enough to coat the back of a spoon. Remove from heat and stir in salt and pepper. Add cheese one handful at a time, stirring until completely melted.

5. Mix pasta and bacon in the casserole dish. Pour sauce over pasta and top with breadcrumbs. Bake for 25 minutes, uncovered. Be careful not to overbake, as you'll lose too much moisture, resulting in a loss of body and creaminess in the sauce. Allow to cool for 10 minutes before serving.

SPANAKOPITA ORZO PIE

SERVES 8

4   ounces orzo

1½   tablespoons olive oil

1   medium onion, diced

2   cups peeled and diced
     eggplant (about half of a
     regular-sized eggplant)

10   ounces frozen spinach,
     thawed, drained of excess
     moisture, and chopped

¼   teaspoon freshly ground
     black pepper

¼   teaspoon sea salt

⅛   teaspoon ground nutmeg

10   ounces feta cheese,
     crumbled

24   sheets of phyllo dough,
     thawed according to
     directions on package

4   tablespoons butter, melted

¼   cup breadcrumbs

Special equipment:

     8-inch springform pan

A LOT OF CHEESE NOVICES SHY AWAY FROM SHEEP'S-MILK VARIETIES. "NO WAY!" THEY cry. "I don't want to try it! It sounds gross!" However, if they enjoy feta cheese, you can wryly inform them that they've already tried it and that, yes, they do indeed like sheep's-milk cheese.

Feta, a traditional sheep's-milk cheese originally produced in Europe and the Middle East, is the star of many hearty dishes. One such dish is spanakopita. Here the standard spanakopita filling—a blend of feta, onions, spinach, and eggplant—is tossed with orzo and wrapped in phyllo to create a delightful little pie. The result is a savory and salty dish with a crisp pastry that collapses into tiny shards at the mere touch of your fork. It's also absolutely darling in appearance, and that alone is enough of a reason to make this recipe.

Many artisan dairies make feta, so use whatever locally produced, high-quality variety you can find. If you have extra filling left over, put it in the fridge and use it the next morning to make the best omelet you've ever eaten.

1. Cook the pasta in a large pot of salted boiling water until al dente. Drain through a colander and set aside.

2. In a large skillet, heat the oil over medium flame. Cook the onions and eggplant, stirring frequently until the onions are soft and the eggplant has taken on some color. Set aside and allow to cool.

3. Toss the onions, eggplant, spinach, pepper, salt, nutmeg, and feta cheese together in a bowl.

4. Preheat the oven to 400°F. Unwrap and unroll the phyllo dough. Be sure to keep it under a damp towel at all times to prevent it from drying and cracking, which will make it hard to work with. To assemble the pie, brush the entire interior of the spring-form pan with melted butter. Layer in a sheet of phyllo dough, gently pushing the dough into the corners of the pan and allowing the edges to hang over the sides. Brush the entire surface of the dough with melted butter and layer in the next sheet of phyllo, rotating this sheet about an inch from the position of the first sheet. Again push the dough into the corners of the pan and allow the edges to hang over the sides. Brush the entire surface of the dough with melted butter. Repeat until all the phyllo has been laid down, rotating each sheet an inch so that the corners fan out in a wagon-wheel fashion, making sure to brush each sheet with melted butter.

5. Spread the breadcrumbs along the bottom of the dough in the pan, then pour in filling and pack tightly. Fold the overhanging edges of phyllo dough over the center of the pie, buttering generously after every two sheets. Bake for 25 to 30 minutes. Allow to cool for 5 minutes before unhooking the springform and serving. » recipe continues

Note: *You can make individual spanakopitas if you desire. To do so, lay out a sheet of phyllo and use a pastry brush to lightly coat the entire sheet with butter. Lay down a second sheet on top of the first and butter that one as well. Place ¼ cup of filling in the center, about 1 inch away from the edge of the dough closest to you. Fold the edges of the dough lengthwise over the filling, so you have one long, narrow rectangle. Brush the surface of the folded phyllo with butter.*

Fold the short edge of the dough up and over the covered filling. Pinch together the filling and the sheets and fold upward into a triangle. Continue folding the triangle shape, applying butter after each fold. Brush more butter on the top and place finished spanakopita on a baking sheet.

Bake the spanakopitas in a preheated 350°F oven for 30 minutes, or until they are golden brown. Allow to cool for 5 to 10 minutes before serving; they are wicked hot right out of the oven. The recipe should yield 12 mini-pies.

ALTERNATIVE CHEESES: Fine feta can be found at many high-end grocers and farmers' markets.

WINE PAIRINGS: Verdejo, white wines from the Greek or Canary Islands

ADDITIONAL PAIRINGS FOR THE CHEESE: olives, watermelon, mint

BAKED ZITI WITH
RICOTTA SOPRAFFINA

SERVES 6 TO 8

- 12 ounces ziti
- 2 teaspoons olive oil, divided
- 1 tablespoon butter
- 1 pound sweet Italian sausage, casing removed, crumbled
- 1 medium onion, chopped
- 2 cloves garlic, chopped
- 2 tablespoons chopped fresh basil
- 1 teaspoon chopped fresh oregano
- ½ teaspoon fresh thyme leaves
- 1 (28-ounce) can crushed tomatoes
- 3 tablespoons tomato paste
- ¼ cup beef or chicken stock
- 4 ounces Pecorino Romano, shredded
- 4 ounces ricotta salata or feta cheese, shredded
- 6 ounces aged Asiago, shredded
- 8 ounces low-moisture (dry) mozzarella, shredded
- 1½ pounds ricotta sopraffina or regular ricotta cheese

ALTERNATIVE CHEESES: Feel free to use Parmesan instead of Pecorino.

WINE PAIRINGS: Sangiovese, Barbera, Nebbiolo, Aglianico

ADDITIONAL PAIRINGS FOR THE SOPRAFFINA: honey, fresh grapefruit, canned peaches, pine nuts

IF YOU WATCHED *THE SOPRANOS*, **YOU PROBABLY REMEMBER EVERYONE IN LA FAMIGLIA** talking about Carmela Soprano's baked ziti. And unless you're Italian—or raised in New Jersey—you probably had no idea what everyone was going on about. It's one of Italy's cheesiest pasta dishes, so we can't figure out why no one thinks of baked ziti when considering the many faces of macaroni and cheese.

This recipe originally came from our good friend Elise Bauer, who just happens to be one of the best home cooks out there. Ziti, a tubular pasta that resembles penne, is baked into hearty layers of cheese and meat sauce before being scooped haphazardly into bowls to make for a hot mess of delicious comfort. Asiago and Pecorino Romano lend the dish their signature saltiness, while ricotta sopraffina—a sweeter, finer version of your standard ricotta—provides a smoothness that regular ricotta just can't muster. *Caro Dio!*

1. Cook the pasta in a large pot of salted boiling water until al dente. Drain through a colander and pour it back into the cooking pot. Toss the noodles with 1 teaspoon olive oil to keep them from sticking, making sure all noodles are coated. Set aside.

2. Heat butter in a large saucepan over medium-high heat. When butter starts to foam, add the sausages and break up any large chunks with a spatula. Cook until well browned, about 6 minutes. Drain off most of the fat from the pan.

3. Stir in onions and cook for 4 minutes, until they are translucent. Add the garlic, basil, oregano, and thyme. Cook for another 2 minutes, stirring constantly. Pour in tomatoes, tomato paste, and stock. Stir well and bring to a simmer. Reduce heat to low and simmer, covered, for 20 minutes.

4. While the meat sauce is cooking, preheat the oven to 350°F. Lightly grease a 9-by-13-inch baking dish with the remaining 1 teaspoon olive oil. Combine the shredded Pecorino Romano, ricotta salata, Asiago, and mozzarella in a small bowl and stir well to combine. Set aside.

5. Once the sauce is done, remove it from the heat and give it a good stir. Stir half of the sauce into the pasta and set the pasta aside.

6. Ladle a thin layer of sauce along the bottom of the prepared baking dish, then dot the surface with half the ricotta cheese. Ladle the pasta into the baking dish, forming a nice even layer. Pour the rest of the sauce over the pasta, creating another even layer, and dot the top with the remaining ricotta. Cover the top with the blend of shredded cheeses and bake until the top is nicely browned, about 30 minutes. Serve immediately.

CHICKEN BREAST STUFFED WITH
LEONORA GOAT CHEESE, STAR PASTA, AND CRUSHED GINGERSNAPS

SERVES 4

- ¼ cup star pasta or orzo
- 8 ounces Leonora, rind on, at room temperature (be sure to ask for a center-cut block)
- 1 teaspoon chopped fresh rosemary leaves
- 1 tablespoon coarsely crushed gingersnap crumbs
- ¼ teaspoon sea salt
- ¼ teaspoon freshly ground black pepper
- 4 boneless chicken breasts, about ¾ pound each (skin optional)
- 2 tablespoons olive oil

  Additional gingersnap crumbs for garnish

  Lemon juice for garnish

Special equipment:

Toothpicks

ALTERNATIVE CHEESES: Monte Enebro, Bûcheron, Zingerman's Lincoln Log, Laura Chenel Chèvre, any solid chèvre

WINE PAIRINGS: dry Rieslings or Gewürztraminers, Crémant d'Alsace sparkling rosé, sparkling rosé Cava

ADDITIONAL PAIRINGS FOR THE CHEESE: strawberry-rhubarb preserves, Medjool dates, fresh mint and basil

WHEN I FIRST TASTED LEONORA, A HEADY GOAT CHEESE FROM THE LEÓN REGION OF Spain, I thought of lemon meringue pie. Yes, really. Tart and creamy with a hint of sweet lemon, Leonora is a refreshing experience. Garrett and I tasted this cheese on many occasions, and each time we were left with a slightly different impression—sometimes strong, sometimes peppery. Miss Leonora is a lady who likes to keep her suitors guessing, but she never fails to please.

This dish is based on a dessert I made as a child: lemon bars with a gingersnap crust. The flavor combination was a revelation to my twelve-year-old palate, so I thought I'd give it a try with a few adult ingredients. Rosemary's signature woodsy notes are just the token of adoration this capricious cheese is looking for, with a zip from spicy gingersnaps adding a playful poke in the ribs. And I swear, every time I watch the star-shaped stelline pasta swirl as I stir the cooking water, I feel like a fairy princess waving my magic wand.   —SS

1. Preheat oven to 375°F.

2. Cook the pasta in a small pot of salted boiling water until almost al dente. (Feel free to imagine yourself a fairy princess while stirring the pasta.) Drain through a colander and rinse with cool water to stop the cooking process. Drain again and set aside.

3. In a small bowl, mix together cheese, rosemary, gingersnap crumbs, salt, and pepper. Gently stir together with pasta and set aside.

4. Butterfly each chicken breast by cutting a deep pocket into the middle of the thickest part of the breast, making sure not to cut through to the other side. Salt and pepper the breasts inside and out. Fill each chicken breast with 2 tablespoons of the cheese-and-pasta mixture, then close the pocket and make sure it stays closed by using the toothpicks to secure the two flaps.

5. Heat olive oil in a heavy-bottomed pan over medium-high heat. One at a time, sear the chicken breasts on all sides and then set in a large baking dish. Once all breasts are browned, slide the baking dish into the oven and cook until the internal temperature of the breasts reaches 155°F. Remember that the middle of the chicken breasts will take longer to cook, because the pasta filling takes longer to come to temperature. Remove the toothpicks and serve immediately, dusted with more gingersnap crumbs and a quick squeeze of lemon juice.

MONTGOMERY CHEDDAR MACARONI
WITH BAKED APPLES

SERVES 4 TO 6

For the apples:

6   **Pink Lady apples (or Honeycrisp or Granny Smith), peeled, cored, and cut into ½-inch chunks**

2   **tablespoons lemon juice**

1   **teaspoon cinnamon**

2   **teaspoons sugar**

    Pinch of salt

For the casserole:

16   **ounces elbow macaroni**

1½   **cups milk**

5   **tablespoons butter, divided**

3   **tablespoons flour**

½   **teaspoon sea salt**

½   **teaspoon freshly ground black pepper**

4   **teaspoons chopped fresh thyme leaves**

20   **ounces Montgomery Cheddar, shredded, divided**

6   **ounces Gruyère, shredded**

3   **cups fresh corn-bread crumbs**

ALTERNATIVE CHEESES: Beecher's Truckle Reserve, Lincolnshire Poacher, any sturdy aged British Cheddar

WINE PAIRINGS: Viognier, Chardonnay, champagne, Pinot Noir

ADDITIONAL PAIRINGS FOR THE CHEESE: chutney, salami, wheat crackers

WHEN I WAS A KID, MY GRANDMA MARINA WOULD SMOTHER A SLICE OF APPLE PIE WITH Cheddar cheese, then slide the plate into the toaster oven to form a thick, orange blanket over her dessert. I was a youngster, so the concept of sweet mixed with savory flavors left me totally baffled. Why would you ruin your sweet treat with a layer of cheese?

Oh, if I had only been able to appreciate the wonderful flavor combination that is cinnamon apples and stout British Cheddar. Something about the sweet heat of the apples and the sharp sassiness of the cheese produces an unexpected pairing that just makes sense. These two strong personalities might be polar opposites, but they fit together like they were meant for each other from the very beginning.   —SS

1. Preheat oven to 375°F. In a small baking dish, combine apples, lemon juice, cinnamon, sugar, and salt. Toss together and cover the dish with foil. Bake for 45 minutes. Once the apples are done, leave the oven on.

2. While the apples are baking, prepare the casserole. Grease a 9-by-13-inch baking dish with a touch of butter. Cook the pasta in a large pot of salted boiling water until al dente. Drain through a colander and spread the noodles into the baking dish.

3. To prepare the mornay sauce, heat the milk in a small saucepan over medium heat. As soon as the milk starts to steam and tiny bubbles form around the edges of the pan, turn off the heat. Place 3 tablespoons of the butter in a medium saucepan and melt over medium flame. Add the flour and stir with a flat-edge wooden paddle just until the roux begins to take on a light brown color, scraping the bottom to prevent burning, about 3 minutes. Slowly add the milk and stir constantly until the sauce thickens enough to evenly coat the back of a spoon—a finger drawn along the back of the spoon should leave a clear swath. Remove from heat and stir in salt, pepper, and thyme. Add cheeses to sauce, reserving 1 cup of the Cheddar, and stir until completely melted.

4. Stir the noodles in the baking dish to loosen them up, then pour the cheese sauce over the pasta and toss until all noodles are coated in sauce. Spread a thick layer of corn-bread crumbs over the casserole and dot the top with the remaining butter. Bake for 30 minutes.

5. Remove casserole from oven and portion onto ovenproof plates. Top each with a heaping spoonful of baked apples and 3 tablespoons of shredded Cheddar cheese, then slide the plates under the broiler for a minute, until the Cheddar on top is a melted, bubbly layer of yum. Serve immediately.

RENNET: VEGETARIAN VERSUS NONVEGETARIAN CHEESES

IT MAY NOT BE APPETIZING TO CONSIDER that many cheeses are developed by combining milk with rennet, the enzyme found in the digestive tracts of farm animals, but it's an undeniable fact of cheese life. Without rennet, we would be seriously limited in the number of cheeses we could produce.

Animal-based rennet, which can come from cows, goats, sheep, or even camels, is integral in the flavor profile of many cheeses. That said, there's a new crop of artisan cheesemakers, particularly in the United States, who are doing impressive things with vegetable-based rennet, which can be sourced from figs, soybeans, papaya, pineapple, thistles, artichoke, or cardoons (which are also known as artichoke thistles, a wild cousin of the domesticated artichoke).

In addition, microbial rennets can be sourced from molds and certain bacteria, while fungi can be genetically engineered to produce enzymes similar to rennet. Both options are vegetarian and very popular with cheesemakers.

Vegetarians may take issue with animal-based rennet, for obvious reasons, and another argument for the use of vegetarian rennet is the high cost and large amount of resources required to produce animal-based rennet. From our point of view, animal- and vegetable-based rennets are simply different tools in the culinary toolbox, and both have produced memorable cheeses. A few examples:

- **CHEESES MADE WITH ANIMAL-BASED RENNET:** Garrotxa, Cantal, Bayley Hazen Blue, Drunken Goat

- **CHEESES MADE WITH VEGETABLE-BASED RENNET:** Humboldt Fog, Vella Dry Jack, Red Hawk, Beecher's Flagship Reserve

CAULIFLOWER AND GRUYÈRE
MACARONI GRATIN

SERVES 4 TO 6

- 1 head of cauliflower, chopped into tiny florets
- 1 tablespoon olive oil
  Sea salt
  Freshly ground black pepper
- 8 ounces elbow macaroni
- 8 ounces Gruyère, shredded
- 1½ cups heavy cream
- 1 teaspoon mustard powder
- ¼ teaspoon ground nutmeg
- ½ teaspoon sea salt
- ½ teaspoon freshly ground black pepper
- 3 ounces Parmesan, finely grated

IF PARMESAN IS THE KING OF CHEESES, THEN GRUYÈRE MUST BE THE QUEEN. A BOLD, nutty paragon of Alpine cheesemaking, this humble Swiss export is praised widely and vociferously.

We decided to show our respect for the queen in the simplest way possible, with a rich winter gratin that flourishes under Gruyère's regal flavor. When roasted, cauliflower becomes incredibly sweet and mirrors the cheese's subtle honey notes. A slight dusting of mustard, Gruyère's most reliable companion spice, rounds the dish out. King Parmesan makes a guest appearance, contributing a crispy crust that accentuates the sultry gratin underneath. All hail the queen.

1. Preheat oven to 375°F. Toss the cauliflower florets with the olive oil and give them a light dusting of salt and pepper. Roast them for 20 to 25 minutes in a 9-by-9-inch pan or a similar-sized casserole dish. The florets should be slightly browned and easily pierced with a fork.

2. While the cauliflower is roasting, cook the pasta in a large pot of salted boiling water until al dente. Drain through a colander and set aside.

3. Pour the pasta into the roasting pan with the cauliflower. Add the Gruyère, cream, mustard, nutmeg, salt, and pepper. Stir until ingredients are well mixed. Use a spoon to push the pasta beneath the surface of the cream and heavily sprinkle the top with Parmesan. Bake for 1 hour. Allow to cool for 5 to 10 minutes so the cream sets before serving.

ALTERNATIVE CHEESES: Comté, Roth's Private Reserve, Beaufort

WINE PAIRINGS: Viognier, Altesse, Roussanne, Pinot Noir, dry rosé

ADDITIONAL PAIRINGS FOR THE CHEESE: toasted walnuts, caramelized onions

SHIRRED EGGS WITH PESTO,
PASTA, AND LAURA CHENEL CHÈVRE

SERVES 6

6 ounces elbow macaroni

8 ounces Laura Chenel Chèvre, coarsely crumbled

12 large eggs

½ cup heavy cream

2 packed cups chopped basil

1 ounce finely grated Parmesan

½ cup pine nuts

2 cloves garlic, roughly chopped

Pinch of sea salt

Pinch of ground black pepper

½ cup olive oil

ALTERNATIVE CHEESES FOR THE LAURA CHENEL CHÈVRE: Foggy Morning, Pipe Dreams Fresh Chèvre, California Crottin, Double-Cream Cremont, Bucherondin, Capricho

ALTERNATIVE CHEESES FOR THE PARMESAN: Piave, Grana Padano, Pecorino, Bianco Sardo

WINE PAIRINGS: Sauvignon Blanc, Grechetto, dry rosés, Malbec, light Pinot Noir

ADDITIONAL PAIRINGS FOR THE CHEESE: roasted beets, fresh or roasted peaches, thyme, rosemary, blackberries, sweet and fruity olive oil

ANY SERIOUS DISCUSSION OF AMERICAN CHEESEMAKING INVARIABLY COMES AROUND to Laura Chenel and the impact she's had on U.S. cheese culture. After learning how to make cheese on a trip to France, Laura began raising goats and making her own chèvre in Sebastopol, California. With a bit of help from Alice Waters, who put in a standing order for it at Chez Panisse, Chenel's creamy, tangy chèvre quickly became legendary. This inspired many other dairy farmers in the United States to produce high-quality goat cheese and led consumers to take notice of previously underappreciated chèvre.

Chenel brand chèvre is perfect in many dishes, including salads, galettes, and hearty macaroni dishes like this shirred mac. Shirred eggs—eggs baked with cream in a small dish—are a breakfast staple for any cook. They're a fine example of elegance found in simplicity, though adding a bit of goat cheese, pasta, and pesto elevates them into a more filling meal. Feel free to use any leftover pasta you have around, for this is a versatile dish that bends effortlessly to the will of the cook.

1. Preheat the oven to 325°F. Grease six 6-ounce (or larger) ramekins with butter and place them on a rimmed baking sheet. Set aside.

2. Cook the pasta in a large pot of salted boiling water until al dente. Drain through a colander and divide equally among ramekins.

3. Divide chèvre among the ramekins, placing it on top of the pasta. Crack two eggs into each ramekin. Divide the cream evenly among all six servings. Bake for 16 to 18 minutes, or until most of the whites are cooked and the egg yolks are barely cooked. The yolks (and perhaps a tiny bit of the whites) should still be a little wobbly. (Don't worry, the residual heat of the pasta will cook them just fine. Plus, the runny yolks act as a sauce that takes this dish up a notch.)

4. While the pasta and eggs cook, make the pesto. Place the basil, Parmesan, pine nuts, garlic, salt, and pepper in a food processor and pulse until chopped. Drizzle in olive oil, processing the pesto until it's smooth but still retains a bit of texture.

5. Once the eggs are done baking, spoon a small amount of pesto into each ramekin and serve. This recipe will make more pesto than you need (unless you really love a lot of pesto, and in that case...God bless you, kindred soul), so feel free to place any extra in an airtight container and use within two days.

PASTA SOUFFLÉ WITH
LEYDEN AND GRUYÈRE

SERVES 6

9   ounces elbow macaroni

3   egg whites

2   cups whole milk

2   tablespoons unsalted butter

2   tablespoons flour

4   ounces Leyden, shredded

4   ounces Gruyère, shredded

3   beaten egg yolks

1   tablespoon chopped chives

½   teaspoon sea salt

Pinch of freshly ground
black pepper

ALTERNATIVE CHEESES:
Marieke's; any well-aged
Gouda and a tablespoon
of toasted cumin seeds
will work.

WINE PAIRINGS: white
Rhône blends, white
wines from the Savoy
such as Chignin or Altesse

ADDITIONAL PAIRINGS
FOR THE CHEESE: roasted
beets, caramelized onions,
rye bread

FLAVORED CHEESES DON'T HAVE THE BEST REPUTATION. SOME CONNOISSEURS SEE THEM as gimmicky cheeses that rely on spices or herbs, not the careful aging of milk, to give them their personality. However, some flavored cheeses have a deep and rich history. Leyden is a traditional Dutch cheese born out of boredom and the spice trade. To perk up their palates, Dutch cheesemakers added cumin to their everyday Gouda to make it more exotic.

Leyden is one of the few flavored cheeses to be lauded throughout the dairy world. Shredded and mixed with Gruyère in this pillowy, poufy macaroni-and-cheese soufflé, Leyden also demonstrates a robust flavor that's strong as cannon fire. Cumin and chives give this dish intrigue, while the soufflé texture is so soft that you can eat it without feeling guilty or overly full.

1. Preheat the oven to 350°F and grease six 6- to 8-ounce ramekins. Cook the pasta in a large pot of salted boiling water until al dente. Drain through a colander and set aside.

2. Using a stand mixer or a handheld mixer, whisk the egg whites at high speed until they become thick and glossy and form stiff peaks.

3. Prepare the mornay sauce. Heat the milk in a small saucepan over medium heat. As soon as the milk starts to steam and tiny bubbles form around the edges of the pan, turn off the heat. Place the butter in a medium saucepan and melt over medium flame. Add the flour and stir with a flat-edge wooden paddle just until the roux begins to take on a light brown color, scraping the bottom to prevent burning, about 3 minutes. Slowly add the milk and stir constantly until the sauce thickens enough to evenly coat the back of a spoon—a finger drawn along the back of the spoon should leave a clear swath. Remove from heat and add the cheeses to sauce, stirring until completely melted.

4. Add the yolks to a small bowl and temper them with the mornay sauce. To do this, slowly ladle ¼ cup of the sauce into the bowl of yolks, whisking vigorously until fully incorporated. Pour the yolks into the mornay sauce. Add the chives, salt, pepper, and pasta, and stir together.

5. Gently fold the beaten egg whites into the macaroni and cheese. Divide among the ramekins and place them on a baking sheet. Bake for 18 to 22 minutes, until lightly golden on top with bits of brown just beginning to form. Be careful not to overbake. Handle gently and serve immediately.

AGED MAHÓN GRATIN
WITH CHORIZO, SHALLOTS, SPINACH, AND CAVATAPPI

SERVES 4

2   tablespoons melted butter

1   package water crackers

10   ounces cavatappi

½   pound dried Spanish chorizo, about 2 large links (Mexican chorizo will also work)

1   teaspoon olive oil

1   cup milk

2   cups heavy cream

1   egg yolk, beaten

½   cup finely chopped shallots (1 whole bulb)

¼   cup chopped fresh parsley

½   teaspoon sea salt

¼   teaspoon freshly ground black pepper

1   pound aged Mahón, rind removed, shredded in a food processor, divided

1½   cups chopped baby spinach

ALTERNATIVE CHEESES: aged raw-milk Manchego, Vella's Mezzo Secco

WINE PAIRINGS: Mencia (Bierzo, Spain), Tempranillo, Muscadet

ADDITIONAL PAIRINGS FOR THE CHEESE: fig nut cake, olive oil crackers, Spanish almonds

AGED MAHÓN IS A WISE OLD SPANISH CHEESE, LIKE AN AGING COUNTRY GENTLEMAN bent over his cane. Firmer than its younger counterpart and with a sharper constitution, the elder Mahón requires only six months to reach mature perfection. And what a difference half a year makes.

This cow's-milk cheese comes from Minorca, and its nutty flavor calls to mind a warm Balearic afternoon, complete with salty sea breeze. But when paired with shallots and spicy Spanish chorizo, aged Mahón takes on heat and vigor. Spinach and parsley provide additional zest, and then there's the *corona de oro*—a thick, insanely crunchy crust made of baked cheese and water-cracker crumbs that you'll need a fork to punch through. *¡Muy delicioso!*

1. Preheat oven to 375°F. Grease a gratin dish with 2 tablespoons butter. There will be extra butter pooled on the bottom of the dish. This is a good thing. Set the dish aside.

2. In a food processor, whiz the water crackers until they achieve a semi-fine texture. Set aside.

3. Cook the pasta in a large pot of salted boiling water until al dente. Drain well through a colander and place in the buttered gratin dish.

4. Squeeze the chorizo out of its casings and break into bite-size pieces. Place the olive oil in a pan over medium heat and cook the chorizo until lightly browned, about 7 minutes. Reserve 2 tablespoons of the fat from the chorizo, discard the remaining fat, then place the sausage crumbles on a plate lined with a paper towel to drain the excess grease. Once drained, toss the meat with pasta in the gratin dish.

5. Add milk, cream, egg yolk, shallots, parsley, salt, and pepper to a saucepan and beat with a fork. Heat over medium flame until the cream reaches a simmer, then add shredded cheese, reserving 1 cup. Remove from heat and stir until melted. Mix in spinach and reserved chorizo fat, return to medium-low heat, and cook for 1 minute, stirring constantly. Remove from heat and pour over pasta in gratin dish. Toss until all pasta is coated with cream.

6. Cover the top of the dish with a generous layer of water cracker crumbs, then sprinkle with the remaining cheese. Bake for 40 to 50 minutes, or until the crackers and cheese are a gorgeous golden brown.

Word to the wise: *Line the bottom of your oven with aluminum foil before preheating. This baby loves to overflow with cheesy goodness, and you'll appreciate the easy cleanup.*

ON THE SWEET SIDE

CHAPTER 5:
ON THE SWEET SIDE

One of the

best parts of being an adult is that you can set your own rules. You don't have to make your bed every single morning, although you might find it's upsetting to your spouse when you don't. You can stay up as late as you want! Or you could if you didn't have work in the morning. And you can drive now! Though that means you're paying for gas, running errands, and driving family members to the airport at all hours of the night.

Oh well, at least you can have dessert first! Definitely one of the benefits of adulthood. This perk can be easily realized through pasta and cheese. You might not expect this combination in a dessert, but is it really so surprising? After all, cheese loves to be paired with dark honey, ripe fruit, and fresh-made jam. Cheese and sugar are a sophisticated—and totally grown-up—match. Think creamy orzo pudding laced with vanilla bean, or coconut-laden Kokos wontons fried and served with caramel sauce.

Of course, you can also make the grown-up decision to share these dishes with your friends, but having first, seconds, and thirds to yourself while you watch reruns of your favorite campy TV show (*Xena: Warrior Princess* and *Firefly* for us, we sheepishly admit) until midnight is also perfectly acceptable. You are an adult, after all. Extra helpings are allowed.

ORZO PUDDING WITH
POACHED DRIED FRUIT

SERVES 4 TO 6

For the pudding:

1   large egg

½   cup plus 2 tablespoons sugar

¼   teaspoon ground cinnamon

¼   teaspoon ground cardamom

¼   teaspoon sea salt

1   vanilla bean

1   tablespoon unsalted butter

1   cup orzo

4   cups whole milk

½   cup full-fat ricotta

For the poached fruit:

2   cups water

¾   cup amaretto (optional; can substitute water with 1 teaspoon almond extract)

½   cup honey

1   large strip of orange peel, about 2 inches wide

1   cup raisins, dried cherries, dried apricots, or other dried fruit

WE'RE HUGE FANS OF CREAMY, WELL-SPICED RICE PUDDING. HOT AND STEAMY FROM the stovetop, it hits the spot on those frigid, snowy nights. Come morning, having had all night to allow the spices to intensify, rice pudding is wonderful served cold alongside a cup of chai tea with honey.

Orzo pudding is quite similar to rice pudding, only a little heartier and less starchy, and with a bit more flavor. Here we lightly toast the orzo before boiling, giving it a pleasant nuttiness. The dried fruit is poached separately to encourage a unique flavor—this recipe relies on the fruits' inherent sweetness to punch up the pudding's milk-and-sugar taste. Be sure to save the boozy poaching liquid, as it is heavenly mixed into a cocktail, especially over ice with a splash of Armagnac or whiskey.

The finished pudding is mixed with ricotta, which adds a slight savory dimension and gives the dish more body. Be sure to use a full-fat ricotta to give your pudding more oomph. You'll find that local, small-production ricottas have more fat and flavor than the large-scale commercial brands available in the supermarket. In fact, a good ricotta is often a sure sign of a small dairy that knows how to handle its milk. If you can get your hands on a buttery sheep's-milk ricotta, well, that's even better.

1. Beat the egg in a bowl and set aside. In another bowl, stir together the sugar, cinnamon, cardamom, and salt. Slit the vanilla bean lengthwise down the middle. Scrape out the seeds with the edge of the knife and add the seeds to the sugar and spices. Set aside. Reserve the empty pod for the fruit poaching liquid.

2. Place the butter in a medium saucepan over medium-high heat. When melted, add the orzo and toast, stirring constantly, for 4 to 5 minutes. The orzo will begin to turn a nutty-brown color similar to that of peanut butter. Don't worry if some pieces of the orzo are darker or lighter than others.

3. Add the milk and bring to a boil over high heat. Once bubbles form around the edges of the milk, remove from heat. Temper the egg by adding 3 tablespoons of hot milk to it, one at a time, whisking quickly. Slowly drizzle the yolk into the milk, whisking constantly. (Adding the egg directly to the hot milk will result in scrambled eggs floating in your pudding. A result that, we assure you, is not palatable in the least.)

4. Add the sugar and spices to the milk, whisking to mix completely. Set over medium heat and bring back to a boil. Reduce heat to medium-low and simmer, stirring constantly, for 18 to 20 minutes. Remove from heat and cool for 30 minutes. The dish will still seem liquidy, about the consistency of hot gravy. Don't worry! It will thicken significantly as it cools. Once it has cooled, fold in the ricotta.

5. As the pudding cools, prepare the fruit. Place the water, amaretto, honey, orange peel, and empty vanilla pod in a small pot. Bring ingredients to a boil over medium heat. Add the fruit to the pot and bring back to a boil. Lower heat to a simmer and cook for 30 minutes. Strain out fruit, reserving cooking liquid for another use, such as drizzling over the pudding or mixing with a bit of vodka. Add fruit by the spoonful to the top of the pudding. Portion and serve.

ALTERNATIVE CHEESES: Any high-quality ricotta will do, but make sure you get the good stuff if you want this dish to truly shine.

WINE PAIRINGS: late-harvest Chenin Blanc, Riesling, Grüner Veltliner, amaretto

ADDITIONAL PAIRINGS FOR THE CHEESE: lemon or orange zest, pine nuts, fruity extra-virgin olive oil

TERROIR AND CHEESE

YOU MAY HAVE HEARD THE TERM *TERROIR* tossed around the artisan food community over the past few years. Rooted in the French word *terre*, "land," it essentially means "the taste of place."

Terroir refers to how a place of origin—and that place's climate, plant life, and soil—affects the flavor of foods that are grown there. Historically used to refer to wine, the word is now used to describe the countless number of ways the natural elements of a food's birthplace can subtly affect its flavor profile.

Cheese is a prime example of terroir at work. Since cheese is made from milk, and milk is made by animals, it makes sense that the taste of a cheese changes depending on the diet of the animals providing the milk. Cheese produced from cattle grazing near the Washington seaboard will taste different than cheese produced from cattle that spend their lives on a Texas hillside. For some, the difference is imperceptible, but if you pay very close attention, you may pick up a nuanced flavor variance. A well-honed palate can almost taste the ocean-kissed grass in chèvre made on the Northern California coast or the chill in the air in an autumn-produced Vermont Cheddar.

FROMAGE BLANC, CHÈVRE,
PEACH, AND GHOST PEPPER CANNELLONI

SERVES 4 TO 6

3 ripe yellow peaches

2 teaspoons unsalted butter

1¼ cups heavy cream, at room temperature, divided

16 ounces Cowgirl Creamery fromage blanc, at room temperature

11 ounces chèvre, such as Laura Chenel, at room temperature

2 cups tart peach jam

Pinch of ground ghost pepper (or ¼ teaspoon ground cayenne pepper)

¼ teaspoon sea salt

20 cannelloni shells

1 teaspoon sugar

¼ cup chopped pistachios

WHEN SWEET RECIPES CALL FOR A CHEESE THAT'S CREAMY AND FRESH, MOST COOKS turn to ricotta, mascarpone, or even cream cheese. I think fromage blanc deserves more attention in the dessert arena. Its salty-tart personality is a perfect pairing for sweet, fruity flavors—especially jam.

Cowgirl Creamery, in Point Reyes, just north of the San Francisco Bay Area, produces one of my favorite varieties of fromage blanc. Made from milk instead of cream, this particular cheese has a less heavy, fatty mouthfeel than some others. The result is a much brighter cheese that, paired with tart chèvre, peach jam, and a micro-pinch of insanely spicy ghost pepper, makes for a swoon-inducing flavor sensation.   —SS

1. Using a paring knife, score each peach with a large X that just penetrates the skin. Fill a bowl with ice water and set aside.

2. Bring a pot of water to boil. You're going to use this same water to cook the pasta later, but do not add salt yet. When the water is boiling, add the peaches and let them bathe for 30 to 45 seconds. Remove them with a slotted spoon and dunk them in the ice water. You should be able to slip the skin right off the peaches. Discard the pits and skins, and roughly dice the flesh of the peaches. Now salt the boiling water, cover, set over medium-low heat, and leave alone until step 6, when you boil the pasta.

3. Preheat oven to 350°F. Butter the bottom and sides of an 8-by-8-inch baking dish and fill the bottom with ⅓ cup of the heavy cream.

4. In a medium bowl, combine fromage blanc and chèvre to make the filling. Mix until thoroughly combined. Stir in peaches and spoon the filling into a pastry bag or a zip-top bag with a small corner cut off.

5. In another bowl, combine jam, ground ghost pepper, salt, and ⅔ cup of the remaining heavy cream, reserving the final ¼ cup of cream for later. Whisk until creamy, then taste and add more of the ground pepper if you want a spicier dish. Set aside.

6. Cook the cannelloni shells in the salted boiling water for 4 minutes, or just until tender. While cooking, make sure to constantly agitate the shells to prevent sticking. Stirring will tear the shells, so just nudge them around the pot with a wooden spoon as they cook. Being careful not to tear the shells, gently drain them through a colander and rinse with a gentle stream of cool water. Carefully shake colander to dry noodles.

7. Using the pastry bag, fill a shell from both ends (half from each end) with cheese filling. Make sure not to split the shells by overfilling with cheese. Set the shell in the prepared baking pan. ❱❱ recipe continues

Repeat with remaining shells, forming a single layer of filled noodles in the pan. Spoon the jam and cream over the top of the shells, making sure to form a nice, even layer over the dish. Slide into the oven and bake for 40 minutes, or just until the top is bubbling gently. Remove from oven and allow to cool for 5 minutes.

8. While the cannelloni are resting, whisk together the remaining heavy cream and sugar in a bowl until the cream holds soft peaks. Top each serving of cannelloni with a generous dollop of the whipped cream and a sprinkle of chopped pistachios.

A note on the ghost pepper: *When we say use a pinch, we really, truly mean one single pinch. Possibly less. Don't go all brave on us and try to squeak in ⅛ teaspoon, unless, of course, you're the culinary equivalent of Evel Knievel. And for the love of God, wash your hands after handling the powder! Any sensitive body parts you happen to touch will thank you. Ahem.*

ALTERNATIVE CHEESES: Any fine fromage blanc will work in this recipe, though we recommend those from Bellwether Farms and Vermont Creamery. For the chèvre, ask your local cheesemonger for a recommendation or use whatever brand you like.

WINE PAIRINGS: lightly sweet sparkling Moscato d'Asti from Piedmont, Italy; lightly sweet sparkling rosé

ADDITIONAL PAIRINGS FOR THE CHEESES: balsamic strawberries, toasted walnuts, honey, English peas, soft-scrambled eggs, bruschetta with basil

SWEET POTATO KUGEL

SERVES 6

- 2 medium sweet potatoes
- 12 ounces full-fat, large-curd cottage cheese
- 4 ounces sour cream
- ¼ cup granulated sugar
- ¼ cup light brown sugar
- 1 teaspoon ground cinnamon
- 1½ teaspoons ground coriander
- ½ teaspoon ground nutmeg
  Pinch of sea salt
- 1 tablespoon vanilla extract
- 3 large eggs
- 4 tablespoons unsalted butter, melted
- 9 ounces egg noodles
- ¾ cup dried cranberries

ALTERNATIVE CHEESES: Any good cottage cheese will work here, though we recommend you use the best you can get your hands on.

WINE PAIRINGS: Moscato d'Asti, Spätlese Riesling

ADDITIONAL PAIRINGS FOR THE CHEESE: golden raisins, candied walnuts, maple syrup, bananas, mangoes, pineapples

KUGEL IS A CLASSIC JEWISH DISH THAT'S SORT OF LIKE A PIE AND SORT OF LIKE A custard, and made with egg noodles. The number of kugel recipes out there is equal to the number of families who think that their recipe is the best on earth, so when crafting a fine kugel, it's all in the hands of the cook to make it unique.

This kugel relies heavily on full-fat, large-curd cottage cheese to make it creamy and give it body. Many local artisan cheesemakers sell cottage cheese and all of theirs will work well here; a good organic brand from your local supermarket will do just fine too. Sweet potatoes and coriander give this dish a November-y flavor reminiscent of sweet potato pie, making it a quirky kugel for your next Shabbat or Thanksgiving dinner. Serve hot or warm, but we also like it cold for breakfast the next day after the flavors have had a chance to mingle. If you have extra spiced sweet potato left over, save it and mix it into pancake or waffle batter.

1. In a pot of boiling water, boil the whole sweet potatoes in their jackets until they are soft and easily pierced with a fork. Remove the sweet potatoes from water with a slotted spoon and place in a large bowl. Allow the potatoes to cool, and then peel off their jackets, which will slip right off in your hands.

2. Mash the potatoes with a potato masher until they are silky, smooth, and completely free of lumps. If you are having a hard time getting the right consistency, place the sweet potatoes in a food processor and pulse until smooth. If you want, you can skip this entire step and used canned sweet potatoes, but the flavor really isn't the same as fresh sweet potatoes.

3. In a medium bowl, mix the mashed sweet potatoes, cottage cheese, sour cream, both sugars, cinnamon, coriander, nutmeg, salt, and vanilla extract until smooth. Beat in the eggs one at a time. Add the butter slowly, while mixing, to fully incorporate. Set aside.

4. Preheat the oven to 375°F. Cook the egg noodles in a pot of salted, boiling water until almost al dente. Strain the noodles and toss in a 9-by-9-inch baking dish with the cranberries. Pour the sweet potato mixture over the noodles—you'll come very close to filling the dish to the top. Gently stir the whole lot of it to get the liquids to sink into all the cracks. You want some of the noodles poking out of the top so the kugel will boast a few delectably crunchy bits.

5. Bake for 60 to 75 minutes, or until set. A knife inserted in the center should come out clean. Let rest for at least 10 minutes before serving.

KOKOS-AND-BANANA FRIED
WONTONS WITH CARAMEL SAUCE

MAKES 60 TO 75 WONTONS

8   ounces Kokos, shredded

2   large bananas, mashed

2   teaspoons dark rum

1   tablespoon brown sugar

2   teaspoons lime juice

1   teaspoon lime zest

60 to 75 wonton wrappers

1   egg, beaten

    Peanut oil for frying

For the caramel sauce:

1   cup granulated sugar

6   tablespoons unsalted
    butter, cubed

½   cup heavy cream

ALTERNATIVE CHEESES:
melted Midnight Moon
or Lamb Chopper plus
1 teaspoon of coconut
extract

WINE PAIRINGS: sweet
sherry, Moscato, cham-
pagne, or forsake wine
altogether and have rum

ADDITIONAL PAIRINGS
FOR THE CHEESE: dark
chocolate, strawberries,
blackberries, thin crispy
water crackers

WE DISCOVERED KOKOS AT THE CHEESE SHOP IN HEALDSBURG, CALIFORNIA. THIS LITTLE storefront carries a vast and eclectic selection of cheeses, but we became especially enamored of this particular Dutch darling. Kokos is made with pasteurized cow's milk in a Gouda style, but it is delicately flavored by the addition of coconut cream. The result is an intensely creamy but firm cheese with the tropical flavor of coconut. It pairs magically with practically all sparkling wines.

Kokos begs to be used in desserts. We've tucked it into wonton wrappers with bananas, rum, and brown sugar, then lightly fried them for an exotic international treat. Served with caramel dipping sauce, this dessert is salty, sweet, and stupid good. We guarantee you there will be no leftovers.

You can find wonton wrappers at any Asian market, but many supermarkets carry them as well. Look in the produce or refrigerated sections. Folding wonton wrappers can be time-consuming, so we recommend you grab a few friends or enlist your children. Trust us, these treats are worth the effort. Your folding minions will agree!

1. Stir together the Kokos, bananas, rum, brown sugar, lime juice, and zest. Place 1 teaspoon of filling in the middle of each wonton wrapper. Use your finger to paint the edges of the wonton wrapper with the beaten egg and fold one corner over to the other, forming a triangle. Press the edges to seal. Paint the two opposite corner points with the beaten egg and then fold them over the center, making a little triangular purse. Repeat with the other wonton wrappers.

2. To fry, fill a wok or heavy-bottomed pan with 2 inches of peanut oil. Heat the oil over medium heat until it reaches 350°F. (Use a candy/fryer thermometer for this; if you don't have one, a nifty trick is to throw a 1-inch cube of bread into the oil. When it turns golden brown in 60 seconds, the oil is ready.) When the oil is at temperature, fry the wontons 4 or 5 at a time for about 90 seconds, or until brown and crispy. Remove from oil using a slotted spoon and cool on a wire rack. Place paper towels under the rack to help make cleanup easy. Set aside and prepare the caramel sauce.

3. Place the sugar in a medium saucepan over medium-high heat. When the sugar has melted, add the butter and whisk in until completely melted. Remove from heat and add the cream, whisking until fully incorporated. Place the sauce in a bowl and dip the wontons.

LA TUR WITH CONCHIGLIE,
NECTARINES, AND APRICOT JAM

SERVES 4

- **2** fresh nectarines, skin intact, cut into ½-inch cubes
- **1** teaspoon sugar, divided
- **10** ounces conchiglie or other medium shell pasta
- **1½** full wheels La Tur, quite ripe and soft
- **¾** cup heavy cream

  A few pinches of fine flaky sea salt

  Apricot jam for topping

LA TUR IS A BRILLIANT CHEESE—AN IDEAL STARTING POINT FOR CHEESE NEWBIES, AND one of our favorite soft varieties. An Italian blend of goat's, sheep's, and cow's milk, La Tur is incredibly rich and buttery, complete with a mild-tasting bloomy rind that many claim is the best part of the cheese.

Given its richness, this small-wheel beauty is well suited for diminutive bowls of pure indulgence. Here, La Tur is paired with the gentle tartness of nectarines and just a touch of apricot jam, producing a dreamy, creamy, sweet-tart experience on the savory end of the dessert spectrum. We enjoy this dish most when it's served after a huge garden salad that has given us the illusion we've earned such a decadent treat.

1. Preheat oven to 350°F. Spread nectarine cubes on a baking sheet and sprinkle with ½ teaspoon sugar. Bake for 5 to 7 minutes, or just until they begin to caramelize around the edges. Remove from oven and set aside. Leave the oven at 350°F.

2. Cook the pasta in a large pot of salted boiling water until al dente. Drain through a colander and fill four 8-ounce ramekins or mini-cocottes with pasta, leaving ½ inch of room at the top.

3. Remove and discard the hardest parts of the cheese rind, keeping the soft, pliable parts. In a bowl, crumble the cheese into small chunks and stir well with a wooden spoon to create an even texture.

4. Place an equal portion of cheese and nectarine into each ramekin and toss gently until well combined. Add 3 tablespoons of cream to each ramekin and give them a little stir. Sprinkle each dish with ⅛ teaspoon of sugar and a tiny pinch of flaky sea salt.

5. Place the ramekins on a rimmed baking sheet and bake for 10 minutes, or until the cream has just thickened into a nice gratin. Slide the baking sheet under the broiler for a minute or two to brown the top.

6. Top each ramekin with a spoon of apricot jam before serving. Serve immediately.

ALTERNATIVE CHEESES: Rocchetta, Langhe della Robiola, Vermont Butter and Cheese Creamery's Cremont

WINE PAIRINGS: off-dry or Kabinett-level Riesling, Chenin Blanc (dry or off-dry)

ADDITIONAL PAIRINGS FOR THE CHEESE: fruit jams, apple butter, Fuyu persimmons

APPENDICES

APPENDIX I: **CHEESE COMPENDIUM**

THE FOLLOWING IS A QUICK REFERENCE GUIDE FOR THE MAIN CHEESES
listed in this book. The list is organized alphabetically by cheese name and
gives details on the milk used in each cheese, the cheese's country of origin,
and the type and/or texture of the cheese (see pages 6–7).

CHEESE	MILK	COUNTRY OF ORIGIN	TYPE
Abbaye de Bel'loc	Sheep	France	Semisoft
Appenzeller	Cow	Switzerland	Semisoft
Barber's English Cheddar	Cow	United States	Semisoft
Beecher's Flagship	Cow	United States	Semisoft
Bianco Sardo	Sheep	Italy	Hard
Brigante	Sheep	Italy	Semisoft
Brillat-Savarin	Cow	France	Surface-Ripened
Bucherondin	Goat	France	Surface-Ripened
Burrata	Cow	Italy	Pasta Filata, Fresh, Soft
Buttermilk Blue	Cow	United States	Blue
Cahill's Irish Porter Cheddar	Cow	Ireland	Semisoft
Camembert	Cow	France	Surface-Ripened
Campo de Montalban	Cow, Goat, Sheep	Spain	Semisoft
Chèvre (General)	Goat	Multiple	Fresh, Soft
Classic Blue Log	Goat	United States	Blue
Cotija	Cow	Mexico	Fresh, Soft
Dolcelatte	Cow	Italy	Blue
Drunken Goat	Goat	Spain	Semisoft
Edam	Cow, Goat	Netherlands	Semisoft
Emmentaler	Cow	Switzerland	Semisoft
Etorki	Sheep	France	Semisoft
Feta	Goat, Sheep	Greece	Fresh, Soft
Fiscalini Bandage Wrapped Cheddar	Cow	United States	Hard
Fontina	Cow	Denmark	Semisoft
Fourme d'Ambert	Cow	France	Blue
Fromage Blanc	Various	Multiple	Fresh, Soft
Garrotxa	Goat	Spain	Semisoft
Gorgonzola	Cow	Italy	Blue
Grana Padano	Cow	Italy	Hard
Grand Ewe	Sheep	Netherlands	Semisoft
Gruyère	Cow	Switzerland	Semisoft
Hoja Santa	Goat	United States	Fresh, Soft
Honey Bzzz Chèvre	Goat	Netherlands	Semisoft
Humboldt Fog	Goat	United States	Surface-Ripened
Idiazabal	Sheep	Spain	Semisoft

CHEESE	MILK	COUNTRY OF ORIGIN	TYPE
Kefalotyri	Sheep	Greece	Hard
Kokos	Cow	Netherlands	Semisoft
La Tur	Cow, Goat, Sheep	Italy	Surface-Ripened
Laura Chenel Chèvre	Goat	United States	Fresh, Soft
Leonora	Goat	Spain	Surface-Ripened
Leyden (Leiden)	Cow	Netherlands	Semisoft
Lincolnshire Poacher	Cow	United Kingdom	Semisoft
Mahón	Cow	Spain	Semisoft
Meadowkaas	Cow	Netherlands	Semisoft
Miticrema	Sheep	Spain	Fresh, Soft
Montgomery Cheddar	Cow	United Kingdom	Semisoft–Firm
Moody Blue	Cow	United States	Blue
Morbier	Cow	France	Semisoft
Mozzarella	Cow, Buffalo	Multiple	Pasta Filata
Nicasio Square	Cow	United States	Washed-Soft
Ossau-Iraty	Sheep	France	Semisoft
Paneer	Cow	India, Multiple Others	Fresh, Soft
Parmesan	Cow	Italy	Hard
Pecorino Romano	Sheep	Italy	Hard
Petit Basque	Sheep	France	Semisoft
Piave	Cow	Italy	Hard
Point Reyes Original Blue	Cow	United States	Blue
Point Reyes Toma	Cow	United States	Semisoft
Quadrello di Bufala	Buffalo	Italy	Washed-Soft
Queso Fresco (General)	Various	Multiple	Fresh, Soft
Raclette	Cow	Switzerland	Semisoft
Red Hawk	Goat	United States	Washed-Soft
Redwood Hill Smoked Goat's-Milk Cheddar	Goat	United States	Semisoft
Ricotta (General)	Various	Multiple	Fresh, Soft
Ricotta Salata	Sheep	Italy	Fresh, Soft
Roaring Forties Blue	Cow	Australia	Blue
Robusto	Cow	Netherlands	Semisoft
Rogue River Blue	Cow	United States	Blue
Roquefort	Sheep	France	Blue
San Andreas	Sheep	United States	Semisoft
Shaft's Blue Cheese	Cow	United States	Blue
Stilton	Cow	United Kingdom	Blue
Taleggio	Cow	Italy	Washed-Soft
Udderly Delicious	Goat	United States	Fresh, Soft
Vella Dry Jack	Cow	United States	Hard
Yodeling Goat	Goat	Netherlands	Semisoft

APPENDIX II: **PASTA GUIDE**

WE USE A WIDE VARIETY OF PASTAS IN THE RECIPES IN this book. Since pasta is the second key component in any macaroni-and-cheese dish, we felt our noodle selection warranted a bit of explanation. In case you can't find the specific pasta called for in a recipe, we've also included a few suitable alternatives.

BUCATINI: Long, slender, spaghetti-like noodles with a hollow center. ALTERNATIVES: Though much shorter noodles, ziti and penne are good substitutes.

CAPELLINI: Also known as angel-hair pasta, capellini looks like very thin spaghetti noodles. ALTERNATIVES: Spaghetti will work just fine, as will linguine. They are thicker but you will get a similar experience.

CAVATAPPI: Short corkscrew-shaped pasta. ALTERNATIVES: Try using fusilli, gemelli, rotini, or other corkscrew-shaped noodles.

CHOCOLATE PASTA: Made with bitter chocolate powder, these noodles can come in many shapes and sizes (see sidebar, Chocolate Pasta, page 42). ALTERNATIVES: None.

CONCHIGLIE: Shell pasta, usually medium-size. ALTERNATIVES: Any shell-shaped pastas will be fine substitutions.

EGG NOODLES: Long, wide, flat noodles that are thicker and chewier than other kinds of pasta. ALTERNATIVES: Any flat, ribbon-like noodles make a good alternative.

ELBOW MACARONI: Standard elbow macaroni, like what you'll see in packaged macaroni and cheese. ALTERNATIVES: While macaroni is a very common pasta throughout the United States, any small noodles, such as wheels or spirals, make decent alternatives.

FARFALLE: Resembles frilly bow ties, and can come in medium or large sizes. ALTERNATIVES: While they are shaped differently, pizzichi or orecchiette are excellent stand-ins.

FARRO: A type of wheat that has a nuttier flavor than the standard flours used to make pasta. Farro noodles come in many shapes and sizes. ALTERNATIVES: Many whole-grain pastas will work in place of farro pasta.

FETTUCCINE: Long, wide, flat noodles that resemble ribbons. ALTERNATIVES: Linguine, egg noodles, or even spaghetti will act similarly to fettuccine in a dish.

FIDEO: Very short, thin noodles commonly used in Spanish cuisine. ALTERNATIVES: Breaking capellini into 1-inch pieces will give you something similar to fideo.

FUSILLI: Long corkscrew-shaped pasta. ALTERNATIVES: Any spiral pasta can replace fusilli, including gemelli, rotini, or cavatappi.

GEMELLI: Spiral pasta that looks like two tubes twisted together. ALTERNATIVES: Use almost any spiral pasta, such as fusilli, rotini, or cavatappi.

IDIYAPPAM NOODLES: Thin, wavy Indian rice noodles that are usually bought frozen and then steamed. ALTERNATIVES: Plain ramen noodles will work in a pinch.

ORECCHIETTE: These little noodles are small pasta disks with a thumbprint in the middle. They resemble small hats or ears. ALTERNATIVES: The shapes are different, but farfalle or other squat, flat noodles can replace orecchiette.

ORZO: Small, rice-shaped noodles. ALTERNATIVES: Any small noodle makes a great alternative. Try stelline or small elbow macaroni.

PENNE: Short, smooth, cylinder-shaped pasta, with the ends cut at an angle. ALTERNATIVES: Ziti, penne rigate, or other short tubular noodles will totally work.

PENNE RIGATE: See Penne, above. *Rigate* simply refers to the grooves that run down the sides of the noodles. ALTERNATIVES: Ziti and smooth penne are fine stand-ins.

PIZZICHI: Short, flat noodles with ruffled edges, similar to small lasagna noodles. ALTERNATIVES: Try farfalle or broken lasagna noodles if you can't find pizzichi.

ROTELLE: Round, spoked wagon-wheel pasta. Usually larger in size, though you may see smaller versions too. ALTERNATIVES: Though they're a different shape, farfalle or orecchiette will work just as well.

ROTINI: Short, flat, tightly wound spiral pasta. This is usually what you see sold as generic spiral pasta at the grocery store. ALTERNATIVES: Fusilli, gemelli, and cavatappi are all structured differently, but they are close enough to act as replacements.

SHELLS (SMALL, MEDIUM, LARGE): Noodles that resemble conch shells. They come in numerous sizes. ALTERNATIVES: Elbow macaroni and shells are easily interchangeable in most dishes. Orecchiette works as well.

SOBA: Long, thick Japanese buckwheat noodles. ALTERNATIVES: Soba noodles are readily available in the international section of many grocery stores. There are not many alternatives to soba, though udon can be a good replacement in some dishes.

SPAGHETTI: Long, thin, round noodles. ALTERNATIVES: Try capellini or linguine if you can't find spaghetti.

SPINACH PASTA: Pasta with spinach added to the dough before forming the noodles. ALTERNATIVES: If you can't find spinach pasta, just use regular noodles. Farro or another whole-grain pasta can work as well.

SQUID-INK PASTA: Pasta made with squid ink, giving it a pleasantly briny flavor. ALTERNATIVES: If you can't find squid-ink pasta, use regular noodles of the same shape called for in the recipe.

STELLINE: Adorably tiny star-shaped pasta. ALTERNATIVES: Orzo, small elbow macaroni, or any other tiny pasta will work well.

UDON: Long, thick Japanese soup noodles. ALTERNATIVES: Plain ramen noodles aren't the same but will work if that's all you can find. You can also try soba noodles.

ZITI: Short tubular pasta, similar to penne, but with the ends cut straight across, not at an angle. ALTERNATIVES: Penne is a great substitute, or try bucatini noodles cut into quarters.

APPENDIX III: **RESOURCES**

CHEESE IS BOTH A SIMPLE AND A COMPLICATED FOOD.
On a basic level, cheese is just fermented milk, but when you get into the types of cheese, methods of cheesemaking, and how a cheese's personality can change throughout its lifetime, things can get overwhelming if you're new to the world of curds and whey. Thankfully, we have a community of incredibly savvy cheese professionals who have taken the time to share their vast knowledge on the topic.

There are many books and websites that can help beginning enthusiasts navigate the finer points of cheese appreciation. Below you will find a handful of resources that will help you better understand cheese, how it is made, and how best to enjoy it.

BOOKS

Cheese: Selecting, Tasting, and Serving the World's Finest
Alix Baboin-Jaubert

Baboin-Jaubert's colorful guide was written for anyone interested in learning more about cheese at the global level. This concise handbook discusses more than three hundred varieties of European cheeses and advises you on the finer points of food and wine pairing, how to build a cohesive cheese plate, and much more. With over four hundred color photos, this book is a joy to behold.

It's Not You, It's Brie: Unwrapping America's Unique Culture of Cheese
Kirstin Jackson

Jackson's jauntily illustrated guide is many things: a cheese cookbook, an American cheese manual, and a narrative journey through the cheese culture of the United States. This accessible handbook will stoke your excitement for fifty notable American cheeses and give you the ability to discuss them smartly with your local cheesemonger.

The Cheese Lover's Cookbook and Guide: Over 150 Recipes, with Instruction on How to Buy, Store, and Serve All Your Favorite Cheeses
Paula Lambert

An icon in the dairy-fermentation world, Lambert's book covers many topics, including buying, storing, cooking, and serving cheese. She walks readers through the art and craft of creating a cheese plate and even offers instructions on making a few varieties at home. At the core of this book, though, Lambert teaches readers to cook with cheese. Her three-page troubleshooting section alone is worth the price of admission.

Mastering Cheese: Lessons for Connoisseurship from a Maître Fromager
Max McCalman and David Gibbons

In this masterwork of cheese writing, McCalman and Gibbons have essentially crafted a textbook for individuals who want to dramatically broaden their knowledge of cheese. *Mastering Cheese* covers everything about cheese, including its history, production, science, laws and regulations, means of preparation and serving, and the authors' top picks of the best cheeses from various regions of the world. Cheesemongers and foodies consider this book an indispensable resource.

Cheese and Wine: A Guide to Selecting, Pairing, and Enjoying
Janet Fletcher

Fletcher takes the classic encyclopedic approach and focuses it on cheese. She lists a variety of top-tier cheeses and provides information on their production, history, and flavor profile. Poetic writing and a defined photographic style make this a popular book for amateur and experienced cheese lovers alike.

Laura Werlin's Cheese Essentials: An Insider's Guide to Buying and Serving Cheese
Laura Werlin

If you're interested in learning how to cook with cheese, Laura Werlin is an incredibly capable teacher. This manual, with fifty recipes that highlight eight different styles of cheese, is a handy guidebook in the kitchen.

CONSUMER MAGAZINES

Culture, the word on cheese:
http://www.culturecheesemag.com

Cheese Connoisseur: The magazine for tasteful living
http://www.cheeseconnoisseur.com

BLOGS

Melt: The Art of Macaroni and Cheese:
http://www.meltmacaroni.com
We built a website to accompany this book, and we filled it
with cooking tips, information about our favorite cheeses,
and, of course, more delicious macaroni-and-cheese recipes.

Cheese Underground:
http://cheeseunderground.blogspot.com
The life and times of Jeanne Carpenter, a self-professed
cheese geek.

Gordonzola: http://gordonzola.net
A San Francisco cheesemonger shares his lovely life of cheese.

Madame Fromage: http://madamefromageblog.com
A cheesemonger extraordinaire explores the lives of cheese
and cheesemakers.

It's Not You, It's Brie: http://itsnotyouitsbrie.com/
Kirstin Jackson discusses all things cheese and explains the
finer points of cheese appreciation.

Serious Cheese:
http://www.seriouseats.com/serious-cheese/
Stephanie's regular cheese column on Serious Eats highlights many favorite cheese varieties with suggestions on
how to enjoy them.

WEBSITES

COWGIRL CREAMERY'S LIBRARY OF CHEESE
http://www.cowgirlcreamery.com/library.asp

THE AMERICAN CHEESE SOCIETY
http://www.cheesesociety.org

IGOURMET'S ENCYCLOPEDIA OF CHEESE
http://www.igourmet.com/st/encyclopedia.asp

I LOVE CHEESE
http://www.ilovecheese.co.uk

MAIL-ORDER CHEESE SHOPS

Artisan cheeses are more readily available than ever before.
Dedicated online cheese shops and specialty gourmet food
outlets are opening every day, and even large-scale chains
like Whole Foods and Wild Oats are investing in the development of cohesive cheese counters. Below is a selection of
retailers that will assist you in finding the cheeses (and pastas)
we've included in this book.

Arrowine
http://www.arrowine.com/
(877) 418-9858

Artisanal Premium Cheese
http://www.artisanalcheese.com
(877) 797-1200

CheeseSupply.com
http://www.cheesesupply.com
(866) 205-6367

Cheese Plus
http://cheeseplus.com
(415) 921-2001

No online ordering, though they
take orders and provide cheese
advice over the phone.

*A passionate cheesemonger is a sign
of a worthwhile cheese counter.*

iGourmet.com
http://www.igourmet.com

Marion Street Cheese Market
http://marionstreetcheesemarket.com   (708) 725-7200

Murray's Cheese Shop
http://www.murrayscheese.com   (888) 692-4339

The Pasta Shop
http://www.markethallfoods.com   (888) 952-400
Yes, they also sell cheese. Lots of it.

Taylor's Market
http://www.taylorsmarket.com   (916) 443-6881

Zingerman's
http://www.zingermans.com   (888) 636-8162

ACKNOWLEDGMENTS

There are a number of people without whom this book would not be resting in your hands today.

First, we must thank Janis Donnaud—our agent, legal adviser, therapist, cheerleader, and friend. She was the first to have faith in us and made sure this book would be successful. Her assistant, Charlotte Kelly, kept us in line and made sure our t's were crossed and our i's were dotted. One thousand thanks to Jaden Hair for introducing us to Janis.

Michael Sand is the most patient and jovial editor we could have hoped for. He's dealt with panic attacks and flurries of e-mails flooding his inbox without warning, and he has immersed himself in new and untested technologies with us. His assistant, Melissa Caminneci, answered our questions and kept everyone sane. In addition, the entire team at Little, Brown did exceptional work in helping us put together this book. Best. Publishing house. Ever.

Matt Armendariz and Adam C. Pearson, our photographer and food stylist, are the force behind the Melt aesthetic. We developed this project with them in mind, knowing that they would bring to light what we saw in our hearts. Without them, this book would be a shadow of its visual self. And to Alexis, Hristina, Beryl, and Eddie: Huge thanks for all of your help in making the shoot happen. Our dishes shone in your capable hands.

Kirstin Jackson, a cheese goddess, wine maven, and dairy editor extraordinaire. Kirstin assisted us with the many pairings that appear with each recipe and was crucial in helping us recommend accessible and brilliant alternative cheeses.

Our copyeditor, Tracy Roe, whose eagle eyes and infinite knowledge of the English language made us look like writers who understand the finer points of grammar and syntax when we usually just fake it.

Many props to Felicia Johnson, a cheese sage like no other, who offered much advice on the subject of categorization and introduced us to many knowledgeable cheesemakers.

A goaty bray goes out to Scott and Jennifer Bice at Redwood Hill Farm, who kindly introduced us to their goats and enviably pastoral lifestyle, and a thank-you to Kathleen Johnson for introducing us to the Bices.

Endless appreciation to Marina Stiavetti and Frances Holm, two mavens of baking whose lives are intricately woven into the roots of this book, whether they realize it or not.

Much love to the ladies of the Cheese School of San Francisco, Kiri, Kristi, and Juliana, for an unbelievably thorough cheese education.

We would not have been able to develop the recipes in this book without the help of a handful of very knowledgeable cheesemongers and their well-stocked cheese counters. Special thanks to the cheese staff of the Pasta Shop in Oakland and Berkeley; Taylor's Market in Sacramento; the Cheese Board Collective in Berkeley; Murray's in New York; The Cheese Shop in Healdsburg, California; and the Campbell, Oakland, and Sacramento Whole Foods Markets. (With a special thanks to Wendy in Oakland!)

Ben de Jesus is our resident web guru: He not only set up the website for the book but helped us with numerous other projects that were beyond our skills. He pulled them off with professionalism and panache. Our gratitude is beyond words.

Special thanks to Le Creuset for its gorgeous cookware. Its casseroles, gratins, and Dutch ovens were integral to the recipe development process.

A number of people helped with research, cheese knowledge, suggestions, advice, proofreading, letting us whine, slapping us upside the head when necessary, or simply being there to eat a lot more mac and cheese than we thought humanly possible. Special thanks go out to Scott Anderson and Blair Mitchell, Carmen Barnard Baca, Elaine Baker, Casey Barber, Elise Bauer, the Bay Area Video Coalition staff, Monica Bhide, Michelle Champlin, Darrell Corti and John Ruden, Alena Filip, Lindsey Givsto, Sandy Grabbe, Nancy Holm, Kris Ide, Dianne Jacob, Dennis Legear, Irvin Lin, Kate Miller, Ken Miller, Jeremy Mosher, John Nelson, Michael Ng, Sarah

Olson, the IT team at Pandora Internet Radio, Peg and John Poswall, Sarah Redman, Ed Roehr, Hank Shaw, Bobby Stiavetti, Amber Stott, Jaime Vela, the ladies of WSBR, Veronica Wunderlich, and the staff at Magpie Café.

Last, we cannot say enough to thank the Army of Melters who kindly dedicated themselves to helping out two people who—in most cases—were almost total strangers known to them only through food blogs. These people are the best cooks, kindest editors, most brutally honest readers, and most ravenous cheese fiends ever to walk the earth: Joy Alegria-Vizcarra, Scott Anderson and Blair Mitchell, Elaine Baker, Rachel Bailey, Emma Bardon, Lexi Beach, Samantha Bennet, Ellen Bird, Erin Blakemore, Michelle Boehm, Heather Bollier-Yetter, Gwen Brass, Nadia Byrnes, Kristen Cederquist, Chris Chrisholm, Sheri Codiana, Susan Covey, Allison Day, Tessa Denney, Blair Diamond, Alexandra Donner, Beth Dreves, Tara Edwards, Janice Espa, Hannah Frey, Lynn Gowdy, Alexandra Grant, Warlie Greiner, Melanie Grigsby, Patrick Guay, Emily Hanhan, Alexis Harmon, Paige Hill, Shannon Huppin, Aislinn Hyde, Susana Jansons, Crystal Johnson, Diana Johnson, Amy Kane, Kelly Kean, Dennis Kercher, Christina Kuratomi, Jacob Little, Kathleen and Tom Loescher, Shilo and Nico Maggi, Lea Marino, Parker Martineau, Allison McKenzie, Karen Merzenich, Diane Miller, Melissa Monge, Susan Monroe, Mimian Morales, Nan Moran, Erin Ohashi, Rachel Olson, Sarah Olson, Trina Palmer, Stefani Pelletier, Peg Poswall, Robin Pridgen, Jenn Reed, Lisa Rogak, Esteban Ruiz, Kate Sandstrom, Holly Scudero, Renee Simon, Sylvia Siu, Jessica Smedley, Sue Smith, Autumn Swindoll, Joanna Taylor, Maggie Trinh, Renate Valencia, Sarah Vanderploeg, Gianluca Verenni, Christina Wells, Joyce Whitney, Andrew Wilder, Laura Williams, Rachel Wilson, Rachelle Woods, Elizabeth Zaffarano, Christina Zambon, Laura Zebehazy, Annelies Zijderveld, and Alexandra Zipkis.

And of course, this book would not exist without the global artisan cheesemaking community. To the men and women who pour their hearts into their curds, hats off to you.

INDEX

Page references in *italic* refer to illustrations.

ABOUT THE AUTHORS

STEPHANIE STIAVETTI is a freelance food writer, recipe developer, and all-around digital-food-media mistress residing in Oakland, California. Her work has been featured in numerous outlets, including NPR, Huffington Post, KQED, Culinate, and Serious Eats. A die-hard tech maven, Stephanie has been blogging since before blogging was invented. You can find her online at TheCulinaryLife.com.

GARRETT McCORD is a freelance food writer, writing teacher, and recipe developer. He has a master's degree in English composition and has written for Gourmet Live, Huffington Post, Epicurious, *Cheese Connoisseur,* and many other online and print publications. You can also find him online scrawling away at his popular food blog, VanillaGarlic.com. He lives in Sacramento, California, with his husband, Brian; their two needy cats; and a Corgi named Jack.